All About The U.S.A.
Region 4

THE HEARTLAND

by
Allan Carpenter

ENCYCLOPAEDIA BRITANNICA EDUCATIONAL CORPORATION

Indexer and Assistant to the Author
CARL PROVORSE

Copy Preparation
VALERIE ROEBKE

Graphic Designer
ISAAK GRAZUTIS

Typography by
LAW BULLETIN PUBLISHING COMPANY

A Word from the Author — Apologia?

One of the author's favorite characters from Lewis Carroll claimed that he could do anything he pleased with words, and with language in general. Over a period of 45 years in publishing, and after 199 books bearing his name, the author at last claims the right to manipulate the language as it pleases him. If he prefers to save his text at the expense of uneven spacing of the paragraphs, he hopes he may do so. If he wants to use an incomplete sentence or to capitalize a word at some time or use a hyphen sometimes and not do either at other times, or to use a hyphen sometimes and not at others—or to use a dash—he now claims the right to do so, by virtue of age, if not senility. It is not often that an author finds editors who are willing to indulge such whims. The editors at Britannica are not only meticulous but also caring, and they have given this author carte blanche in the production of a work which is based on his 45 years of specialized study of the states. So, if such eccentricities and inconsistencies appear in this work and if blame should fall, the author wishes it to be known that he accepts all blame as well as credit, if any.

Copyright©1987 Encyclopaedia Britannica Educational Corporation
All rights reserved   Printed in the United States of America

This work is protected under current U.S. copyright laws, and the performance, display, and other applicable uses of it are governed by those laws. Any uses not in conformity with the U.S. copyright statute are prohibited without our express written permission, including but not limited to duplication, adaptation, and transmission by television or other devices or processes. For information regarding a license, write Encyclopaedia Britannica Educational Corporation, Chicago, Illinois 60611.

ISBN 0-8347-3389-7
Library of Congress Catalog Card Number 86-080847

(Opposite) The Chicago skyline

Contents

The Heartland—Overview 5
Illinois 13
Indiana 27
Iowa 41
Michigan 55
Minnesota 69
Missouri 83
Ohio 97
Wisconsin 111
Index 125
Acknowledgments 128

THE HEARTLAND

FASCINATING REGION

Just as the heart pumps life into the body, the eight great states of the Heartland Region have infused lifegiving wealth into the nation.

Those states produce more than twice the wealth of manufacturing and almost three times the agricultural wealth of any of the other regions in this series.

In the region are some of the greatest transportation centers of the world.

Many of the ideas of modern architecture have emerged from the region as well as many of the nation's greatest leaders in politics, art and music.

The people of the region are far less "homespun" and far more "cosmopolitan" than their countrymen on the east and west coasts imagine them to be.

Life in the area has been far from dull.

One of the nation's great cities was founded by a thirteen-year-old boy. At an even younger age, another boy began his great medical career as an anaesthetist at the age of nine.

The science of medicine was further advanced by a man with a hole in his stomach.

Two notable Winston Churchills are entangled in the life of one of the states.

One of the major cities started life as a Pig's Eye. A much smaller community was christened with watermelon juice and was the first of many American towns to bear the name of a great president.

These are just a few of the unusual facts which make a mighty region come alive.

(Opposite) The Heartland

THE SWEEP OF GEOGRAPHY

Two of the greatest river systems of the continent have their beginnings in the region and a third commences along the border.

The mighty St. Lawrence river system is considered to have its source in the St. Louis River, in Minnesota. Flowing into Lake Superior, the St. Louis initiates the mighty flood which empties all of the Great Lakes into the Gulf of St. Lawrence.

From the time its lower reaches were discovered, explorers had tried to find the source of the majestic Mississippi River. Finally a picturesque exploring party solved the puzzle when the group reached a lake in Minnesota.

The third great river system drains much of the northern interior of the continent into Hudson Bay. This is the Red River of the North, which starts on the Minnesota border and forms that border until it flows north into Canada.

Another important river, the Ohio, does not form in the region, but it flows for most of its length along the southern border of the region.

By far the largest surface of the Great Lakes lies within the borders of six of the states in the region. Only two other states touch those magnificent bodies of water, which form the world's greatest concentration of fresh water.

With one exception, all of the Great Lakes share their shores with Canada. That exception is Lake Michigan, which pours out its enormous benefits to four states of the region.

Geography and history combine in this rare painting by German artist Henry Lewis of the encampment of the Dacotah Indians on the site of present Winona, Minnesota

Another large body of water, Lake of the Woods, is shared by Minnesota and Canada.

Names of the lakes within the states are not so well known, but the lake regions of Minnesota, Wisconsin, and Michigan are unsurpassed for their beauty and sports. Some of the best-known artificial lakes have been formed by the rivers in Missouri.

That state also boasts some of the most notable of all the world's springs, including the largest single-outlet spring in the world.

There are no mighty mountains in the region, but the land is far from drab and flat. Portions of the Ozarks in Missouri and Illinois, as well as highlands of northeast Minnesota, give a mountainous look and provide most of the recreation and entertainment of their taller counterparts.

Old Rib Mountain in southern Wisconsin withstood the mightiest force of the glaciers and still dominates the scenery of its area.

The rocky cliffs and boulders of Lake Superior's northern shore and the towering bluffs of the Mississippi add further scenic variety.

Few journeys anywhere can match the quiet beauty of travels up and down the historic shores of the Mississippi and Ohio rivers.

More geographic variety is added by such unexpected attractions as the Wisconsin Dells and the magnificent panoramas seen from Illinois' Terrapin Ridge.

A SWEEP OF HISTORY

Some of the mightiest works of early prehistoric peoples have been found in the region. How did such primitive peoples manage to raise the great heaps of earth left behind by the Mound Builders? In Illinois alone there are more than 10,000 of these mounds. Monks Mound in Illinois is thought to be the largest primitive earthwork ever built.

Other prehistoric people of somewhat later times developed surprising degrees of civilization. The mounds raised by the Hopewell people show that they knew some advanced methods of construction. Items found in the mounds indicate that the people carried on trade with regions perhaps as far away as Central America.

The most northerly traces of the Aztecs of Mexico have been found in a village in present Wisconsin thought to have been occupied by Aztec immigrants. These technically advanced but fierce cannibal people were hated and probably destroyed by their Indian neighbors.

The Indian groups living in the region when the first European explorers arrived ranged from the woodland peoples of the eastern portions of the region to the prairie groups on the western borders.

As the European population grew along the coast, the stronger and more advanced groups, such as the Iroquois, began to move into the region, forcing the local groups to move westward. There were many terrible clashes over this struggle for territory.

However, one of the striking examples of peaceful agreements among "nations" was found in the pipestone

Artist Charles Bird King painted the striking portrait of Chief Black Hawk

quarries of Minnesota. Here all tribes were free to come in peace to chip away the beautiful stone from which peace pipes, often of great beauty, were carved.

Most of the earliest European explorers came across the Great Lakes from French Canada. However, the British soon began to push in from the east. Of course, the two nations were determined to fight for their claims to the rich territories. These battles of the two countries, each assisted by their Indian allies, finally ended in 1763 when the French gave up their claims to North America east of the Mississippi.

During the Revolutionary War the surprising strategies of George Rogers Clark helped to assure the new nation's

7

Currier and Ives captured the drama of the dynamic life of the period with this Mississippi steamboat race

claim to much of the region. Grants of land to the soldiers of that war helped encourage settlement.

Missouri, Iowa, and parts of Minnesota were added to the nation with the purchase of Louisiana Territory.

Not until the American successes in the War of 1812 did the British give up their hope of regaining control of much of the region. Detroit was not finally brought under American control until 1813.

Ending of Indian wars, tremendous growth in population, the rise of major cities, enormous gains in transportation, agriculture, and manufacturing transformed the wilderness in little more than a generation.

Even the last states in the region to be admitted, Iowa and Minnesota, had grown enough to provide prodigious numbers of men and supplies for the Civil War, as did the other regional states.

Missouri was the only state in the region to suffer major battles. The bloody battle of Westport "saved the west for the Union." Several states were plagued by Confederate strikes and by guerilla raiders who made life a nightmare, particularly in Missouri.

After the war, each state progressed, and historic occasions were noted at an ever faster rate.

By strange coincidence terrible fires swept Chicago, and parts of Michigan and Wisconsin on the same day in 1871.

A rebuilt Chicago created the most splendid of all world's fairs in 1893, and St. Louis followed in 1904.

The region's inventors were busy with such world-altering inventions as the automobile, typewriter, and airplane.

In one of the great engineering feats, Chicago reversed the flow of its river.

The factories of Michigan, Ohio, and Illinois turned out incredible quantities of supplies to help win the two world wars.

Depressions, prosperity and recessions came and went. Some of the worst floods were endured on the Ohio and Mississippi rivers.

A quiet group of men changed the world by achieving atomic power. A more peaceful mission brought the Pope in 1979.

Notable politicians from the region scored triumphs or went down to defeat, as did Walter Mondale in 1984.

All of this and much more combine to make the fascinating story of the eight states of the U.S. Heartland.

A CONCENTRATION OF WEALTH

The advantageous location of all the states in the region on the great waterways—the central position of Chicago, St. Louis, and Detroit in railroad, air, highway and water transportation—provided easy transportation for crops and manufactures and travelers.

Some of the richest iron ore ever found, huge supplies of coal, copper, salt and other minerals provided the raw materials for factories of varied types.

Chicago has boasted the greatest concentration of varied manufacturing to be found anywhere. Detroit became world headquarters for the auto industry, and other Michigan communities led in breakfast food and furniture. The total

THE ECONOMY

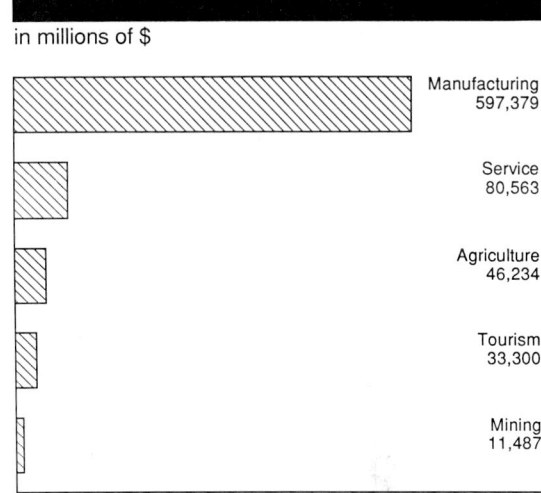

in millions of $

Manufacturing 597,379

Service 80,563

Agriculture 46,234

Tourism 33,300

Mining 11,487

value of manufactured products in the region far surpasses all others.

The rich soil pushed down by the glaciers provided the ideal condition for basic crops, now grown with the most scientific methods available, far outdistancing other regions.

PERSONALITY PLUS

Twelve presidents of the United States have been born in or closely associated with the region. These include Abraham Lincoln, Ulysses S. Grant, William Henry and Benjamin Harrison, Herbert Hoover, Gerald Ford, Harry Truman, Rutherford B. Hayes, James A. Garfield, William McKinley, Warren G. Harding and William Howard Taft.

Others notable in political office or for their attempts to gain office include Adlai Stevenson, Wendell Wilkie, James "Tama Jim" Wilson, Henry A. and

Ulysses S. Grant—brilliant general—frustrated president

Henry C. Wallace, Hubert Humphrey, and Robert M. La Follette.

Some of the most important inventions and scientific discoveries have come from Thomas A. Edison, the Wright Brothers, Christopher Sholes, Cyrus H. McCormick, Dr. James Van Allen, and many others.

Few regions could boast so many major merchants, such as S.S. Kresge, Harry Gordon Selfridge, J.C. Penney, Montgomery Ward, Potter Palmer, Joyce Hall, Joseph Hudson, and Marshall Field.

Industries range from the mighty automobile empires created by Henry Ford and others to the mighty brewing empire of the Busch family and a host of others in various fields.

Creative talent includes the unique architecture of Frank Lloyd Wright, the music of W. C. Handy, the paintings of Grant Wood and Thomas Hart Benton and the writings of Carl Sandburg, Ernest Hemingway, James Whitcom Riley, Booth Tarkington, Lew Wallace, James Michener, F. Scott Fitzgerald, Mark Twain, Paul Laurence Dunbar and Zane Grey.

A wide variety of entertainers have called the region home, including Lillian Russell, John Wayne, Johnny Carson and Buffalo Bill.

Tecumseh, Little Turtle and Black Hawk must be ranked among the best known of the nation's Indian leaders.

Notable personalities include such diverse figures as Mamie Eisenhower, the Doctors Mayo, Charles Lindbergh, Jane Addams, Johnny Appleseed, and General John J. Pershing.

PEOPLES

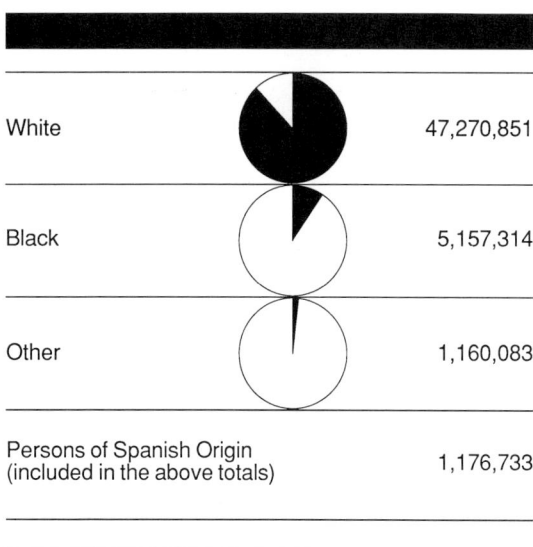

White		47,270,851
Black		5,157,314
Other		1,160,083
Persons of Spanish Origin (included in the above totals)		1,176,733

TRAVELERS' CHOICE

The attractions of the region range from the eerie stillness of Isle Royale and Superior Quetico wilderness to the bustle of many of the largest cities, from the water wonderlands of Michigan, Wisconsin and Minnesota to the craggy peaks of the Ozarks, the banks of Wisconsin Dells or the Falls of Minnehaha, and the charm of Door County.

Some of the world's finest museums include perhaps the greatest of all natural history museums, the Field Museum in Chicago, as well as the Natural History Museum at Milwaukee, the Cleveland Health Museum, the Dearborn Museum, Chicago's Museum of Science and Industry and Art Institute.

More specialized are the Living History Farms at Des Moines and the Circus Museum at Baraboo, Wisconsin.

In the field of music the Chicago Symphony and the St. Louis Symphony have been ranked one and two in the country by leading authorities. Cleveland, Cincinnati, Kansas City and Indianapolis have ranking symphonic organizations.

Chicago has long been a world leader in development of architecture, with many notable examples including the world's tallest building, the Sears Tower. Wisconsin's architectural shrine is Taliesin, home and school of Frank Lloyd Wright. The town of Columbus, Indiana, has gained world fame for its unique buildings by international architects.

The region's presidents have been honored by museums and libraries at their various birthplaces, many of them

Chicago's old Water Tower and Hancock Center on the right (above) and Field Museum (below)

11

"Big Mac" bridge provides a majestic entry into the north country, and restored Fort Michilimackinac offers a tantalizing glimpse of the past

clustered in Ohio, and others ranging from Ford in Michigan to Hoover in Iowa and Truman in Missouri.

Historic communities include Kaskaskia, Galena and Nauvoo in Illinois, Mineral Point in Wisconsin and New Harmony in Indiana. At Dearborn, Michigan, Henry Ford brought together a wide variety of historic structures and called his striking creation Greenfield Village.

A wide variety of annual events draws thousands of visitors to the tulip festivals of Holland, Michigan, and Pella, Iowa, the Winter Carnival at St. Paul, the Indianapolis 500 auto race, the Veiled Prophet Fair at Kansas City, the Jesse James Festival at Liberty, Missouri, and the Paul Bunyan Carnival at Bemidji, Minnesota.

One of the world's most notable monuments is the Perry Monument at Put-In-Bay, Ohio. The statuary of Monument Circle in Indianapolis is also outstanding. Chicago has one of the most notable of all collections of outdoor monuments, including great works by Picasso, Calder and Chagall.

An unexpected center of art is the village of Nashville, Indiana.

As one visitor to the Heartland summed up, "What more could anyone want?"

ILLINOIS

FASCINATING ILLINOIS

Illinois is known as the Land of Lincoln, and there are many fascinating things about Abraham Lincoln's connection with Illinois which are not generally remembered. These include the strange plot to steal Lincoln's body, the only town named for the great man during his lifetime and the only town anywhere to be restored in honor of one man alone.

But there are many other fascinating things about Illinois. Strangely, it once was part of Virginia. Chicago almost became a part of Wisconsin instead of Illinois. In another twist of geography a small part of Illinois is actually west of the Mississippi. Illinois has three of the world's five tallest buildings. One Illinois man was responsible for more "revolutions" than anyone else in history.

Then, just for good measure, Illinois has one of the world's greatest mysteries about prehistoric peoples, and an event in Chicago changed the world.

These are just a few things that make Illinois especially interesting to read about. Taken as a whole, the story of the great state is even more interesting.

THE FACE OF ILLINOIS

The land now called Illinois has been "buried" many times. It was covered over and over by ancient seas, as the land rose and fell, propelled by great forces underground. In later times it was almost entirely covered by the immense sheets of ice called glaciers. The latter happened on four different occasions.

The northwest corner and the very tip of the state were the only parts that escaped the icy layers. The great weight of ice shaved off hills, carved valleys, scooped out lakes and brought layers of rich soil from the north.

When the ice melted, huge inland seas were formed, and the rivers were many times their present size. Lake Michigan is all that remains from the much larger lake of the last ice age, which was known as Lake Chicago.

Much Illinois history has to do with its many great rivers, the mighty Mississippi on the west, the Wabash on the east, the Ohio on the south and the vital Illinois in the center, forming the lifeline of the state.

Illinois has no mountains, but there is a picturesque area of rocky hills in the south, known as the Southern Ozarks. Most of the state is quite flat, except for the bluffs of rivers.

EARLY DWELLERS

Neither the Indians nor early settlers understood the many mounds of earth

---

THAT'S CURIOUS:

Illinois lies east of the Mississippi River. Right? Well, mostly. When Illinois' first capital city, Kaskaskia, was washed away by the Mississippi, the Father of Waters changed its course, leaving an island to the west of the old boundary. If the boundary had been changed to follow the new course of the river, Kaskaskia would now be in Missouri. However, this small chunk of land west of the main river was left as the only part of Illinois west of the Mississippi.

(Opposite) NHAP/EROS provides a dramatic view of Chicago. (Above) Geography and history combine in the view of the Mississippi cliffs and the mysterious Piasa Bird, from an early painting

found in the state, although they knew they were man-made. Monks Mound near Cahokia ranks with the largest works of primitive man around the world. No one is sure how primitive peoples without machinery were able to pile up such enormous amounts of earth.

Some of the 10,000 mounds scattered about the state were given the shape of birds, animals, and snakes. Many of the mounds have yielded skeletons, pottery and other remains which tell the scientists a good deal about these people, known as Mound Builders. Some things found in the mounds must have come from distant places, showing that the people of Illinois traded with far lands even in those days.

Later, because of its good hunting, Illinois was popular with many Indian tribes, but they came and went frequently. Early explorers found six major

THAT'S CURIOUS:

A thirty-foot bird on a cliff! When explorers Marquette and Jolliet rounded a curve on the Mississippi, they saw this huge figure, painted in bright colors. Later, a German artist made a painting of it so we know about how it looked, but its origin remains one of the great mysteries of Illinois history. When the cliff was blasted away for railroad ballast, this prehistoric treasure called the Piasa Bird disappeared forever. Today, modern explorers can see a reproduction painted on a remaining cliff by the people of nearby Alton.

tribes, including the Illini, who gave the state its name. That name means "The Men." They proudly said they were better than all the others.

As time went by, some of the strong Indian tribes were driven from the East and took over much of Illinois. There were the Potawatomi, Ottawa, Piankeshaw and Mascouten. From the north came the Fox and Sauk. Few of the six tribes remained.

STIRRINGS

The first Europeans known to have visited Illinois were famed explorers Father Jacques Marquette and Louis Jolliet. Sent by the Governor General of Canada to explore the Mississippi, Marquette and Jolliet met with the Indians of Illinois and were often feasted by them.

The Europeans had difficulty in eating the Indians' fried dog, and could hardly bear the Indian custom of feeding their guests by hand, like infants.

The explorers followed the entire course of the Illinois River northward, then into the Des Plaines and Chicago rivers. They wrote that the land was very good for settlement, particularly because the rich soil would not have to be cleared of many trees and could grow crops almost at once.

Other French explorers followed Marquette and Jolliet. Robert Cavelier, Sieur de La Salle, known as La Salle, built forts for the fur trade. Until 1699 not a single European settlement had been built in the entire Mississippi Valley. It is strange that the first one was not at the mouth of the great river but in far off Illinois where French priests established Cahokia in that year.

Founded in 1703, Kaskaskia was the most important French settlement in the area, and Fort de Charters became known as the mightiest fortress in all North America. There were never very many French settlers in Illinois. They did some farming and much trading, but after they were driven out by the British in 1765, not much was left of French influence except a few names, such as Des Plaines, Paris, and Marseilles.

The British paid little attention to this remote area, but they did send George Rogers Clark to Illinois to protect settlers from the Indians and the bandits, who made the region an early day "wild west."

When the American Revolution came to the East, there seemed to be almost no way frontiersmen of Illinois could defend the vital western portion of the colonies. However, Clark was an amazing man. He and his men captured Kaskaskia in the name of Governor Patrick Henry of Virginia, who proclaimed Illinois to be a county of distant Virginia.

In the spring, Clark expected the British to march out of Vincennes, Indiana, and recapture Kaskaskia. Knowing the British would never suspect an attack in the middle of the severe winter, Clark and his pitifully small army of 175 men marched through the snows and bitter swamps in one of the great military treks of all time, and surprised and captured Vincennes.

Due to Clark's skill and daring, the entire region to the west was saved from British control during the Revolution.

In 1809, the new country created Illinois as a territory; many settlers came in, mostly down the Ohio River, taking lands the Indians claimed. In the War of 1812 many Indians sided with the

Galena today looks much as it did in earlier times

British, hoping to reclaim their homelands.

During that war, there was a little palisade, known as Fort Dearborn, on the shores of Lake Michigan, where Chicago now stands. Because it was so weak, the U.S. government ordered the fort abandoned.

The men, women and children marched out with the soldiers, and before they had gone far they all were killed by the Potawatomi Indians, an action known as the Fort Dearborn Massacre.

GROWING FAST

After the war, settlers streamed into Illinois, most of them still coming down the Ohio River. Soon, it appeared, Illinois would have enough people to become a state. Without Illinois delegate to Congress Nathaniel Pope, the state would not have had a critical shoreline of Lake Michigan. At his urging the northern boundary was moved 40 miles beyond the southern tip of Lake Michigan. Except for Pope's foresight, Chicago would have been in Wisconsin. With this and other compromises, Illinois was admitted to statehood on December 3, 1818.

With Shadrach Bond as the first governor and Kaskaskia as the capital, Illinois began life as a state.

Indian unrest continued, especially among the Sauk and Fox tribes, as they resisted being moved out of their homelands. The little conflict led by Chief Black Hawk and known as the Black Hawk War was the last Indian war in the state.

Coming of the steamboats on the

Lincoln as a young man

Ohio River brought new settlers and trade to the state at a more rapid rate, but the opening of a water route from the East into Lake Michigan, by way of the Erie Canal, in 1825 created the greatest excitement of all. The little settlement of Chicago was so favorably located that soon much of the water traffic began to funnel into it, and it grew amazingly.

But at one time the river town of Nauvoo was even larger than Chicago. Founded by the leaders of the Mormon Church, at its peak Nauvoo had more than 20,000 population. Joseph Smith, leader of the Mormons, and his brother were mistrusted by their neighbors. After the Smiths were killed by a mob, the Mormons left and Nauvoo became a ghost town.

Another lively town of about the same period was Galena. It became a "western" style mining boom town when its lead (called galena) was making the community wealthy. It, too, was once the largest city in Illinois, but it declined to almost nothing when the lead boom burst.

As the state grew, so did a young settler named Abraham Lincoln. He became convinced that the nation could not be kept together if half its states were permitted to hold slaves. He was able to proclaim his ideas so clearly that he gained nationwide fame, and, of course, became President in 1861. His nomination at the convention center known as the Wigwam in Chicago must be considered one of the highlights of Illinois history.

THAT'S CURIOUS:
Only one town was named for Abraham Lincoln during his lifetime. When told about the plan to honor him, Lincoln said he never had known anything named Lincoln that amounted to anything. However, he brought a wagonload of watermelons to the dedication ceremonies, squeezed some watermelon juice into a cup, poured the juice on the ground and said, "I christen thee Lincoln." Then everyone had a watermelon feast, and a new Illinois town came into being.

Lincoln's opponent for President was another renowned Illinois man, Senator Stephen A. Douglas. This was the only time the two major candidates for President have come from the same state.

Although Illinois was unprepared when the Civil War came, it quickly made up for lost time. Illinois men and women played many heroic roles. Illinois' own Ulysses S. Grant became the Union's chief military man, and finally was able to lead the North to victory. One of the most famous actions of the war was made by Illinois General Benjamin H. Grierson, who led his raiders through most of the South.

The greatest leader of them all, Abraham Lincoln, was reelected in 1864,

The outpouring of grief upon the death of Lincoln demonstrated the great affection of the American people

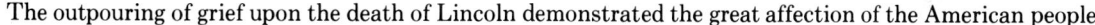

Favorite son, General U.S. Grant, watches over Galena

but he was never again to see his own state alive. After his assassination, his body was returned to Illinois in one of the saddest and most extraordinary processions in history.

MATURING

In 1869 General Grant became the second President from Illinois.

Two years later, Mrs. O'Leary's cow became famous. The Chicago fire probably was not started when the cow kicked over a lantern, but it was the greatest such calamity in the nation's history up to that time. Much of the city was destroyed, but with help from around the world it became bigger and better in record time. Some rebuilding had already begun before the wreckage had cooled.

By 1893 Chicago had recovered so well it held what was perhaps the greatest of all world's fairs—the World's Columbian Exposition. Here electric lighting was used extensively for the first time, and the beautiful buildings and grounds gave the American people a new idea of what they could accomplish.

For that fair, George Ferris invented a new amusement ride, a great wheel turning around with huge cars carrying dozens of people in each one. This ride was copied all over the world, and Mr. Ferris became responsible for more "revolutions" than anyone else.

The fair inspired Chicago architects; Chicago became the home of the first true skyscraper, and the city has been a leader in architecture ever since.

A MODERN STATE

Illinois endured a world war and a great depression, during which Chicago celebrated with another world's fair—the Century of Progress, in 1933 and 1934.

During World War II, a Chicago group was responsible for an event that changed world history. Physicists at the University of Chicago discovered a means of tapping the power of the atom, and the Atomic Age began.

Chicago and Illinois welcomed the opening of the St. Lawrence Seaway in 1959. This made possible a new route for ocean-going ships to come into the port of Chicago.

Less welcome were the events of the Democratic convention of 1968, when rioters made the city notorious around the world.

The 1970's saw the opening of the Sears Tower as the world's tallest building and the death of long-time Chicago Mayor Richard J. Daley.

Chicago's history was enlivened by another mayor, when the city elected its first black chief executive in 1983. Mayor Harold Washington became the center of much controversy as he attempted to activate the reform program he promised in his campaign.

PERSONALITIES

Abraham Lincoln must rank with the best-known personalities of modern history in a way equalled by few others. Lincoln was not born in Illinois, but he grew to maturity in the state and there made the reputation which brought him the presidency.

His experiences flatboating on the Mississippi to New Orleans and in the Black Hawk War broadened his outlook. As an Illinois legislator and brilliant lawyer, his reputation grew. National attention came when he had a series of debates in Illinois with renowned Senator Stephen A. Douglas, who defeated Lincoln's Senate bid. After Lincoln went to Washington, he never returned to Illinois, but he always considered it home.

Illinois' only other President was Ulysses S. Grant. During much of his life he considered himself a failure. His success as the North's leading general took him to the White House, where, again, he came to be considered a failure because he was unable to manage the problems of corruption in his administration. When he retired to Galena, he had financial problems and died thinking he was forgotten by his countrymen.

A distinguished political career which fell short of the presidency was that of Adlai E. Stevenson, who was the Democratic candidate twice, losing to Dwight Eisenhower. He served as Governor of Illinois, and made a reputation as U.S. Ambassador to the United Nations. His grandfather, also Adlai E. Stevenson, was also Governor of Illinois.

Many merchants and industrialists have made Illinois famous. These include Potter Palmer, Marshall Field and A. Montgomery Ward. The inventor of the reaper, Cyrus H. Mc Cormick and Pullman car inventor George Pullman were renowned for their accomplishments.

Nobel Prize winner Jane Addams often has been called one of the greatest women of her time. Writers Carl Sandburg and Ernest Hemingway, another Nobel winner, and Pulitzer winner Gwendolyn Brooks have given Illinois

PEOPLES

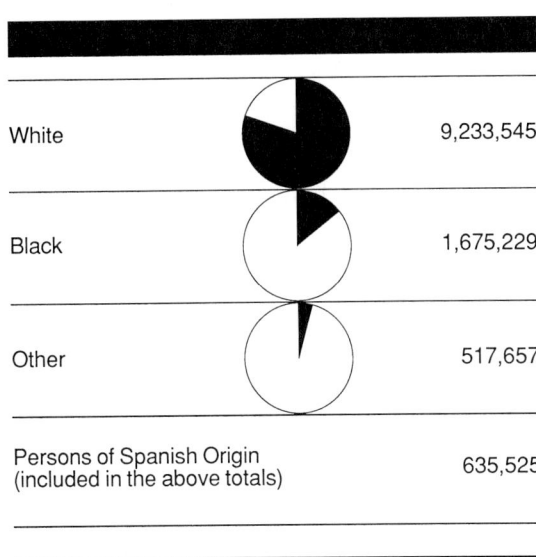

White	9,233,545
Black	1,675,229
Other	517,657
Persons of Spanish Origin (included in the above totals)	635,525

literary distinction, as has publisher John Johnson.

A WEALTH OF NATURE

When the four glaciers deposited a thick rich covering of soil over most of Illinois, they gave the state one of its greatest natural advantages. This fertile flatland has become one of the most productive areas on earth.

Illinois coal reserves still rank very high, but the coal contains so much sulphur that its use has become limited because of the smoke. Oil is still being pumped in southern Illinois, and there are important deposits of limestone, sand and silica sand, from which glass is made.

With Lake Michigan at its doorstep and the many rivers of the state, Illinois is apt to take its water resources for granted. However, the abundant supply of fresh water above ground and the vast underground aquifers give Illinois an advantage over many of the other states. Rainfall, too, generally proves to be just about right for the state's needs.

Much of the original forest was cut for lumber and to clear the land; however, the state still grows more timber than it uses each year. A large part of the state was covered with tall waving prairie grasses, including hundreds of types of flowering plants. Most of these prairies are gone, but a few acres have been preserved to show what such natural beauty was like. More than 2,400 kinds of plants can still be found in Illinois.

The herds of buffalo are gone; now the largest animals are the plentiful deer. More than 180 types of fish tempt anglers to Illinois streams and lakes. Lake Michigan had once been considered "dead" because so much sewage and chemicals had killed the fish. However, as the lake was cleaned up, coho salmon were stocked in the small streams leading into the lake. Now coho and other fish are becoming abundant once again.

USING THE WEALTH

Illinois ranks fourth among the states in farm income. However, it usually is first in soybean production and first or second in corn. Because of the grain grown in Illinois and surrounding states, Chicago has become one of the world's most important grain markets.

The specialty "crops" are interesting. The tiny community of Pana is known for the more than sixty acres of roses growing under glass in area greenhouses, making it the cut rose capital. Belleville has become the focus of the bleached asparagus industry. Mattoon leads the world in broom corn production.

Illinois usually is second to Iowa in hog production and holds high rank in most other fields of livestock and dairy products and poultry.

When oil production in Illinois began to decline, it appeared the state might be out of the oil business, but new means were found to get the oil out of the ground. One method was to pump salt brine into the old wells. This also provided a use for the large salt deposits found in the state.

Illinois has dropped in coal production but it still ranks fifth among the states.

Less well known is fluorspar. Illinois leads all others in producing this vital mineral for rocket fuels and other uses.

With John Deere, International Harvester, J.I. Case and other giants, Illinois continues to lead the world in output of farm machinery. Chicago still ranks as the nation's leading manufacturing center. In fact, 75 percent of all products made in Illinois come from the Chicago area.

Chicago holds first place in at least 20 different kinds of products, and puts out the widest range of other items.

Perhaps most important, Chicago must be considered the premiere transportation center of the world. Other cities may have higher rank in a given means of transport, but Chicago's high rank in most fields of transportation gives it the total lead.

Location, of course, is the key to this leadership. Lake, canal and river transport were first. As railroads came into being, Chicago sprang to the lead and has never been outpaced. O'Hare Airport clears more passengers than any other. With the opening of the St. Lawrence Seaway, Chicago's importance as a port on the Great Lakes was assured.

Traffic on other waterways, highways, and pipelines also is heavy. East St. Louis, Illinois, is one of the great centers for oil and gas pipelines.

In the field of communication, Chicago was a pioneer in both radio and television programming, but it lost this leadership to the east and west coasts.

GETTING AROUND

Chicago has lost out to Los Angeles as "second city" in population. However, this has done nothing to diminish the attraction the great metropolis has for visitors.

THE ECONOMY

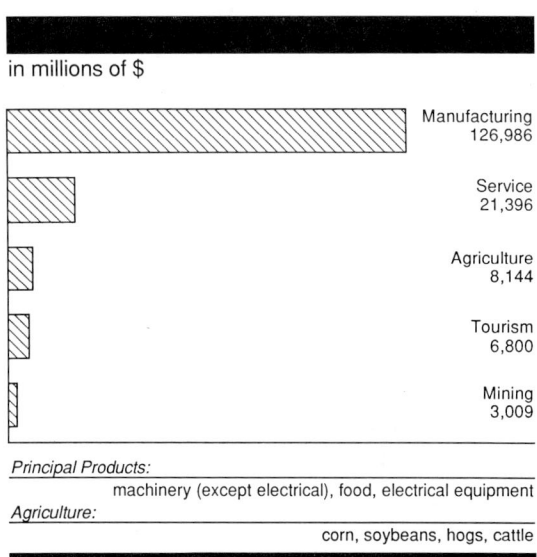

in millions of $

Manufacturing 126,986
Service 21,396
Agriculture 8,144
Tourism 6,800
Mining 3,009

Principal Products:
machinery (except electrical), food, electrical equipment
Agriculture:
corn, soybeans, hogs, cattle

The city's concentration of zoos and museums, great and small, could keep a visitor occupied for weeks. Lincoln Park has the largest free zoo in the world, and Brookfield Zoo was the first in the U.S. to place many of its animals in natural settings.

The Field Museum of Natural History ranks among the top of its kind in the world. It was a pioneer in the type of natural-setting display called diorama. Shedd Aquarium has been called the largest and most complete in the world.

The Museum of Science and Industry was the first of its kind and ranks among the largest anywhere in attendance. The

THAT'S CURIOUS:

People with a sweet tooth should be thankful for the candy factories of Chicago. One out of every four candy bars made in the nation comes from Chicago makers.

The Picasso sculpture at Daley Center, Chicago

Art Institute has a vast collection, with leadership in many fields. Collections of the Oriental Institute are outstanding in the works of the Middle East.

Chicago area museums include others in such special interests as Chicago history, Africa, Poland, Ukraine, peace, lapidary, bicycles, plates, automobiles, trolley cars, and others.

For nature lovers, the Morton Arboretum and the Horticultural Society Botanic Gardens are among the finest.

Chicago has become a city of outdoor sculpture known around the world. When Picasso sent his enormous steel "woman" to the city, he began a trend by the best-known artists. Chagall did a four-sided mosaic on a concrete form a half-block long. Nearby, Calder created a fantastic "Flamingo."

The sculpture of Buckingham Fountain has been known for several generations, and crowds flock to see the changing colors on its 100-foot-high jet. Bertoia's mammoth steel rod sculpture at the Standard Oil Building actually makes a singing sound in the wind.

In music of another kind, the Chicago Symphony is often considered to be the best in the world. Lyric and other opera companies and several ballet groups perform the widest variety of dramatic works.

The Chicago area is known as the world center of modern architecture, with the early works of Frank Lloyd Wright and the pioneering of such giants as Ludwig Mies van der Rohe. The Baha'i Temple in nearby Wilmette is uniquely beautiful.

Only Chicago and New York have two major league baseball teams. Chicago also has teams of major rank in football, basketball, soccer and hockey.

No other state has devoted so much of its sightseeing attention to any one man as that of Lincoln in Illinois. The route covered by the Lincoln family from Indiana to Illinois is the Lincoln National Memorial Highway, with its beginning marked by a bronze statue of young Abe.

The family settled at Decatur; Lincoln's father and stepmother then moved to Charleston, but Abe moved to New Salem alone. This extremely popular historic attraction is the only entire community ever recreated in memory of one man.

Lincoln owned only one house, and this Springfield place has been made to look as it was when the family was there.

24

In Oak Ridge Cemetery, Springfield, the body of the great President lies with those of his wife and sons, except for Robert Todd Lincoln.

Lincoln, of course, never saw the splendid present capitol at Springfield, completed in 1887 at a cost of $4,500,000.

Many of the attractions of Illinois are found in its almost 100 state parks and memorials. The great principal mound and the many other mounds at Cahokia Mounds Park provide the most imposing remains of prehistoric peoples in the country.

Kaskaskia Bell State Park marks the memory of the first capital of Illinois. Nothing remains of its buildings which were washed away in a Mississippi flood. Now a memorial building on the site displays the "Liberty Bell of the West." Older than the Philadelphia Liberty Bell, this bell was rung to celebrate George Rogers Clark's capture of Kaskaskia from the British.

In the State Park bearing its name, the largest stronghold on the continent of its time, Fort de Chartres has been restored to some extent. Local Indians hold a famous powwow there every Labor Day weekend.

Lincoln's tomb and sculpture

COMPAC-FACS

ILLINOIS
The Prairie State

HISTORY
Statehood: December 8, 1818
Admitted as: 21st state
Capital: Springfield, founded 1821

OFFICIAL SYMBOLS
Motto: State Sovereignty, National Union
Slogan: Land of Lincoln
Bird: Cardinal
Insect: Monarch butterfly
Flower: Native violet
Tree: White oak
Song: "Illinois"
Mineral: Fluorite
GEO-FACS
Area: 56,400 sq. mi.
Rank in Area: 24th
Length (n/s): 381 mi.
Width (e/w): 211 mi.
Geographic Center: Logan, 28 mi. ne of Springfield
Highest Point: 1,235 ft. (Charles Mound)
Lowest Point: 279 ft. (Mississippi River)

THAT'S CURIOUS:
In 1874 a gang of counterfeiters made an attempt to steal Lincoln's body from the great tomb, hoping to exchange the corpse for the freedom from jail of one of their members. The plot failed due to the alertness of the Secret Service.

The Illinois capitol, dome and rotunda

Mean Elevation: 600 ft.
Temperature, Extreme Range: 137 degrees
Shorelines: Mississippi River, 518 mi.; Ohio River, 113 mi.
Mountain Ranges: none
POPULATION
1984 estimate: 12,426,000
Rank: Fifth
Density: 205.3 persons per sq. mi.
Percent urban: 83.3%
Principal Cities: Chicago, 3,005,072; Rockford, 139,712; Peoria, 124,160; Springfield, 99,637; Decatur, 94,081; Aurora, 81,293; Joliet, 77,956; Evanston, 73,706
EDUCATION
Schools: 5,220 Elementary and secondary
Higher: 157
VITAL STATISTICS
Births (1980/83): 180,423
Deaths (1980/83): 97,688
Hospitals: 240
Drinking Age: 21

INTERESTING PEOPLE
Abraham Lincoln; Jane Addams; Stephen A. Douglas; Ulyssess S. Grant; Black Hawk; George Pullman; Carl Sandburg; Ernest Hemingway

WHEN DID IT HAPPEN?
1673: Marquette and Jolliet explore
1699: First European town, Cahokia, founded
1765: Rule passes from French to British
1818: Statehood
1839: Springfield becomes capital
1860: Lincoln nominated in Chicago
1871: Fire devastates Chicago
1893: World's Columbian Exposition
1900: Engineers reverse Chicago River
1933: Chicago's Century of Progress
1942: Atomic power becomes reality
1968: State's Sesquicentennial
1970: Latest constitution adopted
1976: Chicago Mayor Richard J. Daley dies
1983: Harold Washington elected as first black Mayor of Chicago

INDIANA

FASCINATING INDIANA

In the not too distant past a man sat on a rock chewing on a bone, and the act became a part of Indiana history in giving a name to a town. In that same town another man was killed by his own "memorial."

Two men associated with Indiana had very unusual associations with hair.

When the state capital was moved to Indianapolis, it was a "Four Wagon State."

Indiana is the home of a disappearing river and plants that eat meat. One of its best-known Indian leaders was credited with making the sun stand still.

A carnival owner once placed a merry-go-round on top of one of the most valuable anthropological sites in the country.

All these and many more contribute to the fascination of the state of Indiana.

THE FACE OF INDIANA

A valuable toehold on Lake Michigan gives Indiana an indirect but practical route to the sea on its northern border. More important for nature lovers, this shoreline is unique in many ways. Wind and sand have formed the Indiana Dunes.

"Here today, gone tomorrow," is the way one naturalist described a "live" dune. The dunes are great mounds of sand. Many of them are covered with vegetation. Those that have no roots to hold them down are carried by the wind from one spot to another.

The wind and the lake have combined

The beautiful Indiana countryside

to create the dunes. Waves bring sand up from the bottom of the lake to the shore. The wind carries the sand inland, piling it up in huge mounds. The combinations of trees, vines, flowers and wildlife of the area make it a "place of beauty unlike any other."

The dunes are a part of the northern lake country, one of the three main geographical regions of Indiana; the others are the central agricultural plain and the southern hills and lowlands.

Eons ago, most of the state's surface was formed by the mammoth forces of the glaciers, which covered all but the "driftless" south-central area. More recently much of Indiana's life, both past and present, has been shaped by the rivers.

The mighty Ohio twists and turns to

THAT'S CURIOUS:
One of Indiana's rivers flows aboveground, then disappears only to rise and disappear several times. The Lost River travels underground for 22 miles.

---

form the entire southern border. The banks of the Wabash River are known in song and story. They form the southwestern border of Indiana.

Most of the average 40 inches of precipitation finds its way to the Gulf of Mexico by way of the Wabash and Ohio rivers. The rest flows through the Great Lakes basin.

The continental divide which separates the waters in that way is not a mighty ridge like the Rocky Mountains, but rather a gentle two-way slope.

Indiana boasts a total of more than 1,200 lakes, clustered mainly in the northeastern part of the state.

EARLY DWELLERS

A little rise of earth was the site of an amusement park merry-go-round until state officials discovered it was a rare "fiddle-back" mound, and they managed to save some of it from destruction.

This was one of the many mounds in Indiana that cover the burial places, fortifications and refuse dumps of the ancient peoples who once lived in the area.

Indiana has a wealth of reminders of the various peoples—Adena, Fort Ancient and Hopewell cultures, as they are known. They left behind examples of their copper work, textiles, basketry, and polished stone. It is thought they had domesticated animals and used the bow and arrow.

By the time European settlement began on the east coast, there were almost no resident Indian tribes in what is now Indiana.

However, when Europeans first became familiar with the Indiana region, they found tribes known as Potawatomi, Miami, Chippewa, Illinois, Ottawa, Wyandot, Shawnee and others. These generally were groups that had been driven west by white settlement in their eastern homelands.

The well-organized Miami had four chiefs for each of the tribes. The chiefs were always equally divided between men and women, even the war chiefs.

Today the principal Indian memories remain in many of the place names, such as Kankakee, Mishawaka, Kokomo, and Wabash, or wa-pe-sha in the Miami tongue.

The name Indiana is the only state name that directly reflects the civilization of the original peoples of the continent.

STIRRINGS

There are strange but partly believable legends of a group of white people from England or Wales who lived on Rose Island about 1200 A.D., but not much credit is given to these accounts.

Samuel de Champlain may have reached the area of Fort Wayne, and other explorers and priests probably visited the area. However, in 1679, Robert Cavalier, known as La Salle, actually came to the St. Joseph River,

(Opposite) Indianapolis by NHAP/EROS

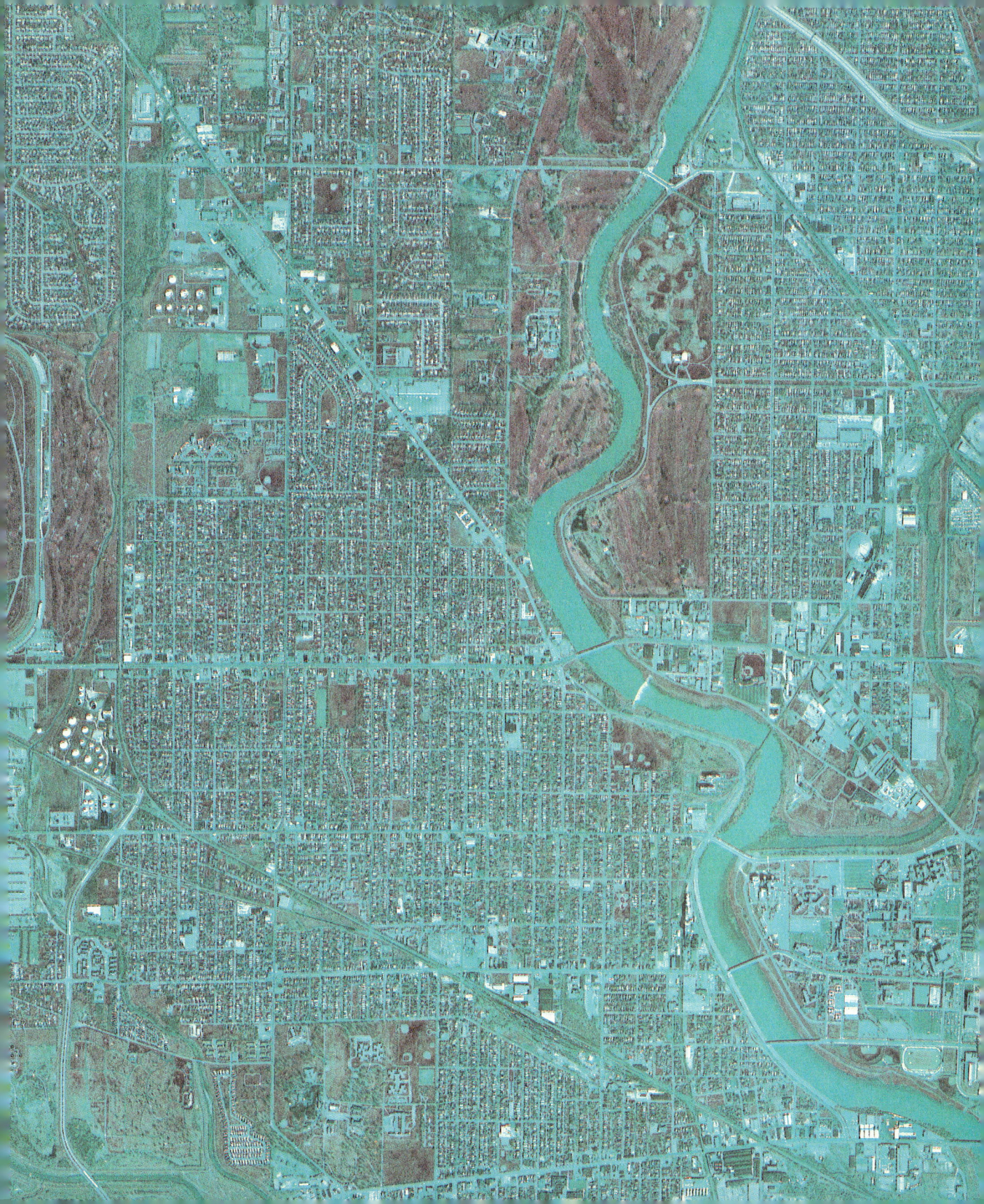

The Prophet Tenskwatawa, portrait by Charles Bird King

near present Benton Harbor, and his party reached present South Bend.

The first French stronghold, Fort of the Miamis, may have been built as early as 1700. Vincennes perhaps was the site of a fort by 1708, and with the coming of settlers, this became the first permanent European settlement in Indiana in 1732; it was established by Francois de Vincennes.

During the early French period, Indiana was particularly important as a route from the French holdings in Canada to their Louisiana territories on the far-distant Gulf of Mexico. The route up the Maumee River, across the portage at Fort Miami, down the little Wabash to the Wabash, Ohio and Mississippi was called the "Glorious Gate."

The many French licensed "voyageurs" traded supplies and trinkets to the Indians in exchange for furs. The happy-go-lucky French settlers mingled freely with the Indians and considered them as equals, often intermarrying.

However, more and more British traders came in, and the British claims to the area were strengthened. The deadly French and Indian War ended in 1763 with the French loss of their North American claims, and the British took over.

In the Proclamation of 1763, the British King placed the lands west of the Appalachian Mountains off limits to settlement. This order was to protect the wilderness and the valuable fur trade. The French settlers remained and managed as best they could.

For the most part the Indians hated the British and often went on the warpath. Chief Pontiac and his army were able to capture forts Ouiatenon and Miami and drive the British from Indiana.

THE REVOLUTION AND OTHER WARS

They did not return until 1777 when British commander Henry Hamilton sent soldiers to Vincennes.

One of the great and little-recognized heroes of the Revolution was the young officer from Kentucky, George Rogers Clark. Because Virginia claimed the whole western area, Clark asked Governor Patrick Henry of that state for help in driving the British out.

Hamilton was sure the Americans would not attack Vincennes during the terrible winter. However, Clark made a desperate march from Kaskaskia, Illinois, toward Vincennes, wading across icy rivers; he and his men were not even able to dry their freezing clothes.

The surprised Hamilton was defeated and captured in "one of the greatest exploits of American arms." Although the Americans could not capture Detroit, Clark's success gave the new country firm claim to the whole region after the Revolution.

Clark and his men received a grant of 150,000 acres, where Clark established Clarksville. This became America's first new settlement in the entire Northwest Territory.

In 1787 the Northwest Ordinance set up rules for governing the vast territory that included present Indiana. By 1790 Governor Winthrop Sargent established an American government at Vincennes.

More alarmed than ever by the taking of their lands, the Indians grouped to drive the Americans out. Under Chief Little Turtle, the Miami Indians defeated General Josiah Harmer at present Fort Wayne, and they went on to other victories.

To overcome the Indians, President Washington sent General "Mad Anthony" Wayne. He had been given this nickname because he made such madly daring moves during the Revolution.

General Wayne trained his troops in the kind of warfare used by the Indians. Just across the border in Ohio he defeated the Indians. At Fort Miami a new fort was called Fort Wayne in the General's honor.

The region was open to peaceful settlement for about 15 years. A very large area was called Indiana Territory, and William Henry Harrison was made the first governor.

George Rogers Clark memorial, Vincennes

The governor gained many Indian lands for settlement through peaceful negotiation. Enough settlers had come in by 1809 so that the present borders of Indiana were set, in a new and much smaller Indiana Territory.

The British had never given up hope of reclaiming all of the "western" lands. They encouraged the Indians to battle the Americans. One of the most notable Indian leaders was Chief Tecumseh, who formed an Indian confederacy headquar-

THAT'S CURIOUS:
In the "bloody year" 1777, Hamilton paid the Indians to bring in the scalps of the Americans. He became known as "Hair Buyer Hamilton."

31

Restored New Harmony keeps its artistic tradition in modern buildings such as the roofless church

tered at Prophetstown, named for his brother, the Indian Prophet.

In a battle along the banks of the Tippecanoe River, the Indians were defeated and Prophetstown destroyed.

A "real" war came in 1812, as the British sought to recapture the west. General Harrison led his forces into Canada and won a victory over British General Proctor and Tecumseh, where the chief was killed.

By the end of the war settlers were arriving in numbers, by 1816 totalling 60,000. On December 11 that year, Indiana became the 19th state.

In the treaty of 1818, the Delaware Indians sold their lands in central Indiana and promised to move west. In 1820 a commission selected a site for a new capital, Indianapolis. It had only two white settlers at the time. By 1825 the new capital was occupied as the seat of state government.

After 1856 only a few Indians remained in the state named for them.

One of the unusual epics of Indiana history is that of New Harmony. Robert Owen was a man with a vision of a perfect society. He established New Harmony as a place where leaders in the arts, sciences and other fields could make a home in the wilderness.

A group of these talented people floated on houseboat rafts down the Ohio River and up the Wabash. Because there were renowned scholars, educators and artists aboard, their craft was called the "Boatload of Knowledge."

Because of the unusual ability of those settlers, the community has been ranked along with other "world villages that have made history."

They experimented in early education, established libraries and trade schools, along with women's clubs. Many scientific advances were made.

One of the great improvements of the period was the 460-mile-long Wabash and Erie Canal, begun in 1832. By this time railroads and other improvements also were coming at a rapid rate.

Indiana's favorite son William Henry

THAT'S CURIOUS:
When the state government moved to Indianapolis, the entire property of the state required only four wagons for the move.

Harrison captured the presidency in 1840, with his slogan "Tippecanoe and Tyler Too," referring to the battle and to his vice presidential candidate, John Tyler.

There had been a few slaves in Indiana, but by 1843 they were gone. Most of the people of the state were opposed to slavery, and many helped slaves to escape over the "Underground Railroad."

Although Indianapolis did not get the honor of holding the Republican National Convention of 1860, it did give Abraham Lincoln 26 votes on the first ballot for President. This may have turned the tide in Lincoln's favor.

When the Civil War came, Governor Oliver P. Morton of Indiana was such a strong supporter of the Union that he came to be called the "nation's strongest Civil War governor."

Indiana reached its quota of Civil War volunteers only five days after the first call was made.

The war itself came to Indiana mostly through such raids as that of General John Hunt Morgan in 1863. There was a small skirmish at Corydon.

It is thought that General Morgan might have captured Indianapolis if he had known how weak it was, but the General swept on into Ohio.

As the war drew to a close, the body of President Lincoln passed through the state on the funeral train, pausing at the capitol at Indianapolis.

A MODERN STATE

The wartime activities had brought considerable prosperity to the state. After the war immigration from many nations introduced new ideas and brought many

Lincoln Boyhood National Memorial

traditions. Indiana has been called "a typical melting pot of cultures."

After ten years in building, the present state capitol was dedicated in 1878. Two years later, Wabash claimed a world title—as the first city to be lighted with electricity.

The state flag came about as a result of a contest. The Daughters of the American Revolution offered a prize for a design to celebrate the Indiana Centennial in 1916. Mooresville's Paul Hadley is the father of the flag.

As America entered World War I, Bethel Gresham of Evansville was one of the first three Americans to die in battle. That war called 130,670 Indiana men and women into service.

Although Indiana is generally thought of as a northern state, during the 1920's

PEOPLES

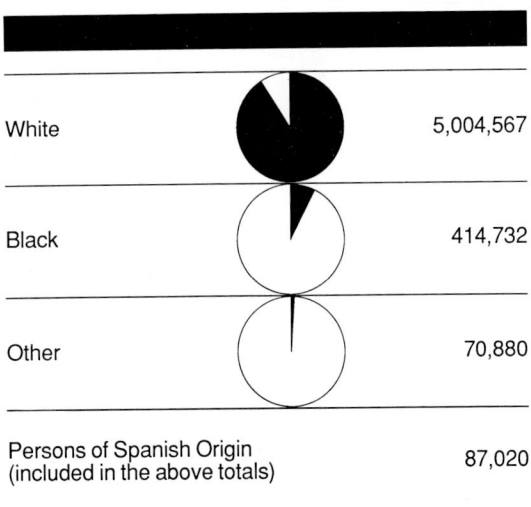

White	5,004,567
Black	414,732
Other	70,880
Persons of Spanish Origin (included in the above totals)	87,020

many people took up the southern cause of the Ku Klux Klan, which opposed blacks and other minorities.

This trend began to die down with the sentencing of a Klan leader for murder.

In 1937 the state suffered the worst floods in history up to that time, with great damage to property.

World War II again spawned wartime prosperity. However, it brought death in the far corners of the world to 10,000 Indiana men and women.

Starting early in the 20th century, the Indiana shores of Lake Michigan have become "...one of the world's great industrial centers," with important concentrations of steel and oil industries.

These industries have cut deeply into the natural wonderland of the dunes areas. In 1966 Congress authorized parts of the remaining dunes as Indiana Dunes National Lakeshore, now covering more than 12,000 acres of this irreplaceable region.

There was room, however, for a badly needed public port; Burns Harbor was developed and began operation in 1970.

In the period between 1940 and 1980 the Indiana population grew by more than 2,000,000. However, between 1980 and 1983 there was a small drop in population.

The Republicans continued their control of the statehouse, as Robert D. Orr began a new term as Governor in 1985.

PERSONALITIES

The number of outstanding personalities developed in Indiana is far out of proportion to its population. This is especially remarkable in view of the relatively short history of the state.

Although Abraham Lincoln was not born in Indiana, and although he moved on to Illinois as a very young man, his frontier life there as a boy helped to shape his personality in many important ways.

When Abraham was nine years old, the Lincoln family moved from Kentucky to Indiana; for some distance they had to cut their way through wilderness to reach their new home near Little Pigeon Creek.

THAT'S CURIOUS:
An Indiana military man is remembered for an unusual cause. General Ambrose Burnside wore bushy whiskers on the sides of his face. These came to be called "burnsides" and then the name became twisted as "sideburns."

All winter long they huddled in a lean-to shelter. Growing up without formal education, Lincoln would walk 17 miles to borrow law books from a law firm library. He worked hard at all the jobs available in the area. His father hired him out to neighbors for 25 cents a day as a baby sitter and laborer.

During his years in Indiana, Abraham Lincoln learned how to study, how to work effectively, and most of all how to get along with people. He was one of the most popular young men in his area. When the family left Indiana, Abraham Lincoln had laid a foundation for future greatness.

Indiana has been associated with other presidents. William Henry Harrison gained his reputation on the Indiana frontier. His grandson, Benjamin Harrison, practiced law at Indianapolis and was a U.S. Senator from Indiana before becoming President.

Elwood native Wendell L. Willkie gained fame as the 1940 Republican candidate opposing F. D. Roosevelt.

During his term as Governor, Indiana's Oliver P. Morton gained national attention for his support of the Civil War effort. When the state withheld funds for the war, Morton borrowed on his own credit to carry on.

He was said to have "held aloft the hands of Lincoln until victory came...a deputy President of the United States." Morton later served in the U.S. Senate until his death in 1877.

Some of the nation's greatest Indian leaders were associated with Indiana. The Shawnee Chief, Tecumseh, has been called "one of America's truly great men." He tried in many ways to give his people a better life. His grand plan called for a nationwide Indian confederacy to drive out the white invaders, but he was defeated by an overwhelming tide of "civilization."

Tecumseh's brother, Tenskwatawa, called the Prophet, gained great fame when he made the sun stand still on June 6, 1806. Of course, he had learned that an eclipse of the sun was due that day. He brought disaster to his brother's cause when, in spite of Tecumseh's warning, he went out to meet General Harrison and was defeated at Tippecanoe.

Chief Meshekinnoquah, Little Turtle, was responsible for what was perhaps the greatest defeat of U.S. forces until Vietnam. He later realized the Indian cause was hopeless and made friends with several American presidents, beginning with Washington.

At his death Little Turtle was given a military burial.

Some of the nation's greatest leaders in the arts have had their roots in Indiana, perhaps more in proportion to population than any other state.

The "Hoosier Poet," James Whitcomb Riley was born in a log cabin at Greenfield. Gene Stratton Porter of Wabash gained fame with her book "A Girl of the Limberlost."

Indianapolis writer Booth Tarkington twice won the Pulitzer Prize for novels, but he is remembered most for another novel, "Seventeen," about teen-age life.

Another Pulitzer Prize winner was historian Albert J. Beveridge, also a U.S. Senator.

Lew Wallace was one of the best-known and controversial figures of his time, as a general, lawyer, and statesman, as well as famed author. As the youngest Major General of the Civil War, his

Johnny Appleseed's grave site

career was clouded by a misunderstanding with General Grant.

Wallace's career took a strange turn when he became a Mexican general. In another career change, General Wallace created the novel "Ben Hur," which became one of the most popular books of its time, later made into spectacular motion pictures. He wrote this work while he was Governor of the Territory of New Mexico. In another unusual turn of fortune, Wallace became Ambassador to Turkey, where he wrote "The Prince of India."

Artist Theodore Steele started tiny Nashville, Indiana, on its way to becoming a noted center of artists and galleries.

Cartoonists Frank McKinney (Kin) Hubbard and John T. McCutcheon gained world fame for their perceptive work.

Two of America's best-known popular songwriters were Cole Porter of Peru, Indiana, and Hoagland (Hoagy) Carmichael of Bloomington.

A WEALTH OF NATURE

Indiana has given its name to one of the world's most popular building stones—Indiana limestone. The state still has large limestone reserves of a type known as oolitic.

As many as 62 Indiana counties still are involved in oil production, and there is known to be a modest amount of natural gas.

Coal, other building stone, brick and ceramic clays, shale, sand and gravel all are abundant.

The plant life of the Lake Michigan dunes is one of that area's most unusual features. Found there are plants like the bog callas of the distant northern lands and the tropical white lizard tail, desert cactus and arctic lichen, orchids and other rare plants.

Tulip poplar, the state tree, is one of Indiana's 134 native tree species. The sycamore is particularly outstanding in the state.

More than half the animals and birds which were found by the pioneers can be

THAT'S CURIOUS:
Two unusual Indiana plants are "meat eaters." The carniverous pitcher plant and sundew lure insects into their interior, capture them with sticky substance and digest them.

seen no longer in Indiana, but some smaller animals and about 160 species of birds may still be found.

USING THE WEALTH

Northwestern Indiana is known for one of the greatest concentrations of industry anywhere. Gary grew around the mammoth U.S. Steel works to become the largest U.S. city founded in the 20th century. Today the state still ranks about third in steel production.

Indiana holds second rank in the printing of books, leads in biological products, prefabricated buildings and musical instruments.

Because more than half of all band instruments are made at Elkhart, the city is known as the band instrument capital of the world. The massive tubas and other "brass" instruments it turns out have also made it the city with a lot of brass.

South Bend has been a leading manufacturing center. Studebaker wagons and automobiles were famous for a hundred years. Other famed autos of an earlier day were also produced in the state.

Fort Wayne has another unusual association with cars. It produces a large part of the world's gas station pumps. The city also holds a leadership position in diamond tools.

Most of the country's magnets are made at Valparaiso, and Indianapolis leads in telephone manufacture.

Muncie turns out the most glass containers, and Anderson factories make the most files for scraping.

Because it can be carved and chiseled so readily, Indiana limestone has long been a favorite with builders. Most of the country's dimensional limestone comes from the area of Bedford/Bloomington.

Coal is the state's leading mineral in dollar value, with petroleum production and processing also very important. The refinery at Whiting is a world leader.

Indiana holds third rank among the states in corn production, but is often first in popcorn. It usually holds second or third rank in soybeans, and third in hogs.

Indiana has long claimed the leadership in the rather unusual field of mint, grown for oils. It ranks first in distilling peppermint and spearmint oils.

Historically, the Ohio River has been, and remains, one of the busiest for shipping. Today's barges pushed by tugs haul heavy products of almost every type. The state's river transportation companies are among the largest anywhere.

THE ECONOMY

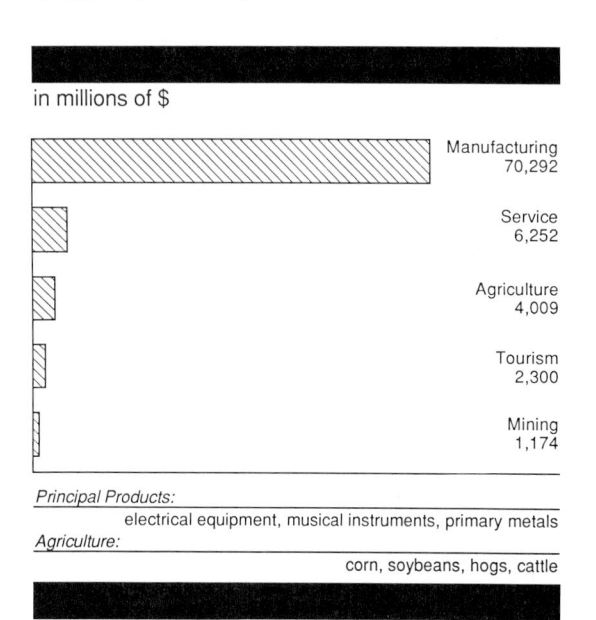

in millions of $

Manufacturing 70,292
Service 6,252
Agriculture 4,009
Tourism 2,300
Mining 1,174

Principal Products:
electrical equipment, musical instruments, primary metals
Agriculture:
corn, soybeans, hogs, cattle

Notre Dame University

In transportation, Indianapolis is one of the nation's central hubs. At one time the city was the greatest center of electric interurban transportation.

GETTING AROUND

The tiny villages of Gnaw Bone and Bean Blossom are among the most-visited places in Indiana. This is because they are located in one of America's great tourist attractions—Brown County. The county's blooming trees of spring and the brilliant foliage of autumn combine with one of the best known of all small towns, Nashville, to attract visitors.

Sometimes their cars line the country roads for miles. Perhaps no other village the size of Nashville has such a collection of art, gift, novelty and antique shops along with well-known eating places. Many of its resident artists are widely known.

Parke County, site of over 30 covered bridges, is popular for its Covered Bridge Festival in October each year.

The town of Columbus may outrank all others of its size for the number and variety of structures noted for architectural quality, and for the famed architects associated with them.

The state's oldest town is Vincennes, named for founding Francois de Vincennes. Its Creole Ball harks back to its French beginnings. Notable structures at Vincennes are St. Francis Xavier Cathedral and the striking George Rogers Clark State Memorial.

New Harmony provides one of the most complete and interesting restorations of an early planned community. Its modern "Roofless Church" resembles an opened parachute. Rappite sect members believed the imprints of human feet on Gabriel's Rock were made by that heralding angel.

Indiana boasts three universities of international fame. Perhaps best known of all is Notre Dame at South Bend. It is renowned for its football team, quality of education, and one of the largest and most beautiful campuses anywhere.

At Bloomington, Indiana University is in the first rank of state universities. Both Indiana University and Purdue

THAT'S CURIOUS:
At Gnaw Bone, John Allcorn was killed by a falling poplar tree. His casket was made from the wood of the tree. The green wood sprouted and grew, the resulting new tree is now a memorial to Allcorn.

University at Lafayette are known for their brilliant musical faculties. The 6,107-seat Elliot Hall of Music at Purdue is one of the world's largest theaters.

Peru calls itself the Circus City and has an annual circus festival. Ben Wallace of Peru bought a carnival with a one-eyed lion and an elephant named Diamond. He built this into the Hagenbeck-Wallace circus, one of the largest of its time.

Johnny Appleseed Memorial Park at Fort Wayne honors the strange but much loved man who planted apple trees that flourished over much of the midwest. Some of these still remain as living memorials.

The capital, Indianapolis, is the country's largest city that is not on a navigable waterway.

Heart of the city is Monument Circle with the soaring Soldiers and Sailors Monument towering 284 feet toward the sky. Dedicated to the enlisted men and women of the armed services, it is thought to be the first of its kind.

Not far to the west of the circle is the grand capitol. It is considered to be the only major public building of its type to be built within its budget.

The five-block-long World War Memorial Plaza was designed to honor the men and women of the state who died during the two world wars. Here is the impressive Indiana World War Memorial. Its Altar Room is dedicated in honor of the American flag. The huge statue called "Pro Patria" stands outside. It is considered to be the largest bronze ever cast in the United States.

The Memorial Plaza also features a tall obelisk and cenotaph. One of those honored in the cenotaph is James B.

Indianapolis 500 auto race, one of the nation's great annual attractions

Gresham, one of the first three Americans to die as a result of World War I. Another imposing part of the Memorial Plaza is the national headquarters of the American Legion.

An unusual museum is the Children's Museum. This is devoted to the special interests of young people. Art and music are represented in the John Herron Art Institute and Clowes Hall, where the Indianapolis Symphony is heard.

Perhaps most widely known of all the attractions of Indianapolis is the tremendous track on which the annual Indianapolis 500 auto race is run. Each Memorial Day, world sports attention focuses on this exciting and sometimes deadly event.

The splendid Indiana capitol

COMPAC-FACS

INDIANA
The Hoosier State

HISTORY
Statehood: December 11, 1816
Admitted as: 19th state
Capital: Indianapolis, founded 1821
OFFICIAL SYMBOLS
Motto: Crossroads of America
Bird: Cardinal
Flower: Peony (paeonia)
Tree: Tulip poplar
Song: "On the Banks of the Wabash, Far Away" by Paul Dresser
Stone: Limestone
GEO-FACS
Area: 36,185 sq. mi.
Rank in Area: 38th
Length (n/s): 276 mi.
Width (e/w): 177 mi.
Geographic Center: In Boone Co., 14 mi. nnw of Indianapolis
Highest Point: 1,257 ft., Wayne Co.
Lowest Point: 320 ft., Ohio River
Mean Elevation: 700 ft.
Temperature, Extreme Range: 151 degrees
Number of Counties: 92
POPULATION
Total: 5,479,000 (1983)
Rank: 14th
Density: 152 persons per sq. mi.
Principal Cities: Indianapolis, 700,807; Fort Wayne, 172,028; Gary, 151,953; Evansville, 130,496; South Bend, 109,727; Hammond, 93,714; Muncie, 77,216
EDUCATION
Schools: 2,552 elementary and secondary
Higher: 74
VITAL STATISTICS
Births (1980/83): 277,000
Deaths (1980/83): 154,000
Hospitals: 133
Drinking Age: 21
INTERESTING PEOPLE
James Whitcomb Riley, William Henry Harrison, Benjamin Harrison, Oliver P. Morton, Wendell L. Willkie, Lew Wallace, Booth Tarkington, Ambrose Burnside, Hoagland (Hoagy) Carmichael, George Rogers Clark, Jonathan Chapman (Johnny Appleseed), Ernie Pyle, Elwood Haynes, Abraham Lincoln, Anthony Wayne
WHEN DID IT HAPPEN?
1679: La Salle traverses
1732: Vincennes established
1763: French hold relinquished
1779: George Rogers Clark wins the west.
1787: Indiana is part of Northwest Territory
1809: Present Indiana established as territory
1811: Harrison defeats Indians
1816: Indiana becomes 19th state
1825: Indianapolis becomes capital
1832: Beginning of Wabash and Erie Canal
1842: Notre Dame University begins
1861: Indiana responds to war appeal
1863: Morgan's Confederates invade
1865: Assassinated President's cortege pauses
1887: Capitol completed
1894: "Modern" auto perfected by Haynes
1905: U.S. Steel establishes Gary
1911: Initial race of Indianapolis 500
1937: Worst Ohio River floods
1940: Republicans nominate Willkie, FDR defeats
1966: Statehood Sesquincentennial celebrated
1970: Port of Indiana at Burns Ditch opens
1976: Indiana Dunes National Lakeshore extended
1985: Republicans continue hold on statehouse

IOWA

FASCINATING IOWA

When the lady on the seat beside him asked where he was from, the man answered that he came from Iowa. "Oh," the lady remarked, "Cleveland, Ohio?"

The incident illustrates the difficulty many people have in locating Iowa or placing the state in their minds. Ohio, Idaho and Iowa sound alike, but of course they are really different and distinctive.

Iowa lacks the mammoth cities, the stupendous scenery and the ocean beaches, but, in some ways Iowa is the most distinctive of the states.

On a more human scale, there are many intriguing things about the state.

There is a lake surrounded by a stone wall, the creek that was set on fire to awe the Indians, the world's longest furrow, the "Calico Railroad," and the distinctive fruit born in a lightning storm.

The history of the state tells of a "war" fought over honey, of the Greybeards who marched in the Civil War, of the famous explorers who were feasted by Indians who placed the food directly in their mouths.

The story includes the Iowa man and woman who were immortalized by a painting but whose names are not recognized, the famous melody that was written on a shirt cuff.

There are even such oddities as the squirrel cage jail, where the prisoners were rotated on a lazy susan.

The "Portrait" of Iowa shows a strong personality that assures a distinctive place in the story of the states.

THE FACE OF IOWA

What do you do with 25 percent of all the grade-A land in the United States? The answer is simple; you use this most valuable treasure of any state to become the most productive area in the world!

When the four different glaciers of the ice age covered most of Iowa, they brought with them those incredible layers of deep rich soil from areas to the north. The glaciers' enormous weight leveled much of the land, leaving it almost perfect for farming.

Only a small portion of Iowa in the northeast escaped the glaciers, now called "Little Switzerland."

Over most of the state the landscape is serene, broken occasionally by the bluffs of the many rivers. The hardwood trees along the rivers turn to spectacular colors in the autumn.

Iowa is secured between the two great rivers, the Mississippi on the east and the Missouri on the west. The Big Sioux River flows into the Missouri and completes the western boundary. There is a total of 600 miles of border rivers.

The Cedar and Des Moines are other major rivers.

There are only about 100 lakes in Iowa, many of them artificial. Okoboji and Spirit lakes are the major natural lakes.

At one time the National Geographic Society called Okoboji the world's third most beautiful lake.

THAT'S CURIOUS:
Iowa has a lake surrounded by a stone wall. During the winter, ice pushes boulders to the shore all around the lake, forming the barrier that gives the lake its name—Wall Lake.

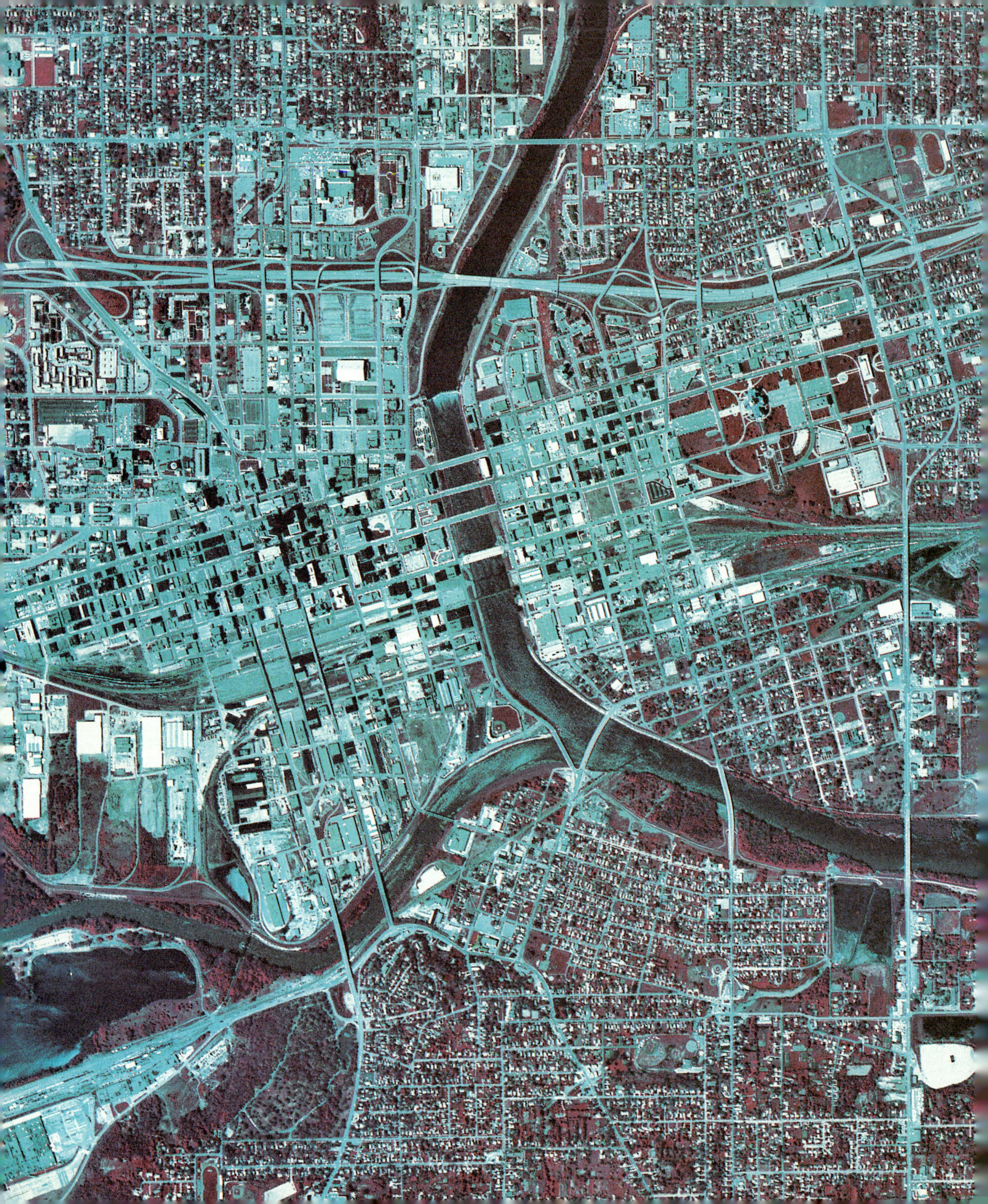

At one time, strangely, the highest point in Iowa was thought to be a man-made point, prehistoric Ocheyedan Mound. New observations place the state's highest point elsewhere in Osceola County.

EARLY DWELLERS

The many mounds heaped up by the ancient peoples thousands of years ago are the most imposing of the many traces they left behind.

Some of the mounds have been formed in the shape of birds and animals. These are sometimes known as effigy mounds.

Effigy Mounds National Monument outside McGregor is the only national preserve in Iowa.

Village sites, rock paintings, and ancient trails are other reminders that people lived in Iowa in ancient times.

The Indian peoples found in Iowa by the early European explorers knew nothing about the earlier peoples.

There were two main groups of Indians in Iowa when Europeans arrived, the Plains Indians and the Woodland Indians.

Plains Indians had occupied the region for generations. The Woodland Indians kept moving farther west as they were being pushed out of their eastern homelands by European settlement. The two groups fought to possess the land.

Although the Ioway Indians gave the state its name, they were never numerous, perhaps not more than 1,500. Other plains tribes included the Winnebago, Osage, Ponca, Omaha, Missouri, Sisseton and Wahpeton.

Among the woodland groups were the Fox, Chippewa (or Ojibway), Miami, Potawatomi, Ottawa and Illini.

(Opposite) Des Moines from NHAP/EROS;
(Above) Bird Effigy Mound

Over the years all of the Indian groups moved or were forced out. The Mesquakie were moved to Kansas, but they longed to return to Iowa. Saving up their government allotments, they were able to buy a tract of land near the town of Tama. They returned, to become the only Indian tribe living in the state today.

STIRRINGS

When the canoes of the exploring party of Father Jacques Marquette and Louis Jolliet passed the mouth of the Wisconsin River, they were the first to enter the mighty Mississippi and the first Europeans to visit Iowa.

Eight days passed before the party dared to come ashore and meet the Indians. They probably landed somewhere near Oakville on June 25, 1673.

Instead of being hostile, the Illini

Indians who met them were very friendly. As a sign of honor they fed the explorers by hand, putting food in their mouths, much to their discomfort.

The Marquette and Jolliet party and others that followed laid the basis for the French claim to the whole Mississippi Valley, but not much attention was paid to the area for nearly a hundred years.

Then, in 1763, France surrendered its entire Louisiana claims to Spain, and present Iowa was included in the grant.

Spain never did much to strengthen its claim. In Iowa the Spaniards gave only three grants of land. A French-Canadian miner, Julien Dubuque, received one of these claims in 1796. He had been living and mining lead in the area of Catfish Creek since 1788.

Dubuque was a master in dealing with the Indians. When they refused him a favor on one occasion, he said he would burn the creek. He had a helper pour some oil on the creek upstream. As it floated down in the night, he set the oil aflame, and the Indians were terrified. Dubuque got his way and promised to put out the fire just as it died down.

EARLY GROWTH

Spain secretly returned the Louisiana region to France. In 1803 France in turn sold the entire area to the fledgling United States.

One of history's greatest expeditions was sent out to explore the new property, headed by Meriwether Lewis and William Clark. They spent thirty days pushing up the Missouri River along what is now the Iowa border. In their entire journey to the Pacific coast and back, only one man of the party died. Sergeant Charles Floyd died a natural death and was buried at the present site of Sioux City.

The first American flag to be raised in eastern Iowa was hoisted by explorer Zebulon Pike, in 1805. A notable high point on the Mississippi bluffs is called Pikes Peak, like its higher namesake in Colorado.

The name Iowa was first used by Lieutenant Albert Lee, who explored the valley of the Des Moines River.

Fort Madison, established in 1808, was burned by the British in 1813 during the War of 1812.

Only fifteen years had passed after the Lewis and Clark expedition had fought its way up the Missouri when the first steamboat reached present Council Bluffs in 1819. This was the "Western Engineer."

With few settlers Iowa had little formal government as it became in turn part of Missouri Territory, Michigan Territory and Wisconsin Territory, with its capital at Burlington in 1836.

As more settlers came in, Iowa was established as a separate territory two years later. Robert Lucas was the first governor.

However, the boundary with Missouri was disputed. Governors on both sides gathered their troops in a dispute over the area. Fortunately, this little civil war

THAT'S CURIOUS:
The Missouri-Iowa border dispute seemed important at the time because wild honey hives were found in so many trees of the area. Sweetenings of any kind were important to the frontier. The dispute has come to be called the "Honey War."

never came about, and the U.S. Supreme Court later decided in Iowa's favor.

By 1836 Dubuque had grown large enough to support Iowa's first newspaper.

Many pioneers were coming in. Since there were no roads, they often lost their way. Dubuque merchant Lyman Dillon hitched his five oxen to a large plow and started out. He never took his plow out of the ground until he reached Iowa City. He had dug the longest continuous furrow ever plowed. Wagon tracks beside the furrow soon made it a well-established road.

When Iowa was admitted to the Union as a state on December 28, 1846, it became the first free state to be carved from the Louisiana Purchase.

Statehood was followed by the first telegraph lines in 1848 and the first railroad in 1853. When the railroad ran out of cash to pay its workers, the workers were given bolts of calico cloth for wages. Not surprisingly, it became known as the Calico Railroad.

The first bridge across the Mississippi was finished in 1856.

The University of Iowa opened its doors in 1855, and that same year the now world-famous colony of Amana was founded.

A year later, the state capital was moved from Iowa City to a brash young town named Des Moines, nearer the center of the state.

Iowa had been a state for only 15 years when the Civil War erupted. Because the state was too poor to do so, Iowa Governor Samuel J. Kirkwood paid

Many groups from Europe brightened the Iowa scene, such as the Dutch at Pella with their annual festival

45

THAT'S CURIOUS:
Iowa fielded one of the most unusual outfits in the history of warfare. Every man in the regiment was over 45; some were much older. Named the "Greybeards," they were not called into battle but served behind the lines.

---

for outfitting the entire First Regiment at his own expense.

Iowa troops played a key part in many battles, particularly the Battle of Iuka and the Battle of Wilson's Creek. Without the Iowans the whole north central region might have fallen.

There were more volunteers from Iowa than could be used, and the draft was never activated in the state. The total manpower from Iowa alone was greater than all of Washington's army.

A MODERN STATE

When Abraham Lincoln visited Council Bluffs in 1859 just before running for President, he decided that town would make a good terminal for a continental railroad. Just ten years later, the first railroad across the continent began to operate through Council Bluffs.

In 1876 the Iowa prairies near Le Mars became home to a group of wealthy English people who bought large farms and lived like country gentlemen.

Nature gained the headlines in episodes at Estherville and Grinnell. The great meteor of 1879 that sizzled across the Estherville sky was one of the largest to have been observed. Its metallic remains were dug up out of deep craters and sold to various museums.

The tornado which struck Grinnell in 1882 proved to be one of the worst ever known.

Grinnell had recovered sufficiently by 1889 to field its football team against the University of Iowa. This was the first intercollegiate football game played west of the Mississippi. In the next few years, Iowa State University became one of the great football powers.

Another sport made world news in Iowa. Only fifty years after its founding, the young state became an international leader in harness racing. The track established by Charles W. Williams at Independence held many world records. Williams became the only man to develop two champion stallions of their class.

Independence had become a metropolitan center, with interurban transport, a grand hotel, and an opera house. But all this glory soon faded in the depression of 1893.

When the Spanish-American War was kindled by the sinking of the battleship Maine, Iowa had a special interest. One of the two officers killed on the Maine was Darwin R. Merritt of Red Oak.

In another and larger conflict, Iowan Merle Hay was one of the first three Americans to die after the country entered World War I.

Iowa seaman J.C. Sabin fired the first American shot of the war. In this first American encounter of that war a German submarine was sunk.

The time after that war saw many improvements. From having almost no paved roads, Iowa built roads at such a fast rate that within ten years it ranked fourth among the states in mileage.

Drought, dust storms and the great depression brought Iowa's farm economy almost to a halt, and many lost farms that had been in families for generations.

Blaming the hard times on Republicans, in 1932 Iowa voters swept the Democratic Party into control of the state for the first time since the Civil War. By 1938, however, the Republicans had regained control.

World War II called more than 260,000 Iowans into service, and 8,398 died in that service.

After the war, farm values and rural prosperity increased for a long period. Nevertheless, during the 1960's Iowa changed from a rural to an urban state, with more people living in the cities and towns than on the farms.

The Democratic Party regained control of the state legislature in 1976, but long-time Republican Governor Robert Ray remained in office.

One of the most notable religious events in the state's history occurred in 1979 when Pope John Paul visited Iowa and addressed huge crowds. At the Living History Farms where the Pope spoke, a church now stands in honor of the occasion.

In the early 1980's farm prosperity began to diminish and with it much of Iowa's prosperity, so dependent on farms. By 1985 farmers claimed the problem had reached crisis proportions. Land values had dropped; many farmers were overwhelmed by debt, and prices were too low to meet expenses. The situation was not expected to improve for several years.

PERSONALITIES

In 1928 Herbert Clark Hoover, a native of West Branch, became the first

Iowa farms are basic to the state's economy

president to have been born west of the Mississippi.

However, both before and after his presidency Hoover had a remarkable career.

As an engineer and geologist, he raised mining standards in Australia, helped make Chinese mines more productive and practiced his profession in nearly a dozen other countries.

During and after World War I, he supervised relief efforts which helped to save thousands made hungry and homeless by war.

As Secretary of Commerce under Harding and Coolidge, he brought new methods of efficiency to American business.

Unfortunately for Hoover, the great depression began soon after he became president. Much of the trouble of the

PEOPLES

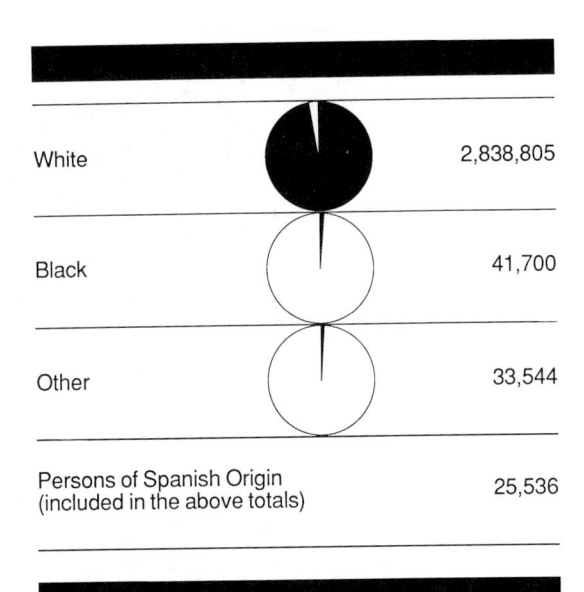

White	2,838,805
Black	41,700
Other	33,544
Persons of Spanish Origin (included in the above totals)	25,536

time was blamed on Hoover. Historians now believe that most of this was unjust. Nevertheless, he served only one term.

In later life he was made chairman of committees for reorganizing the federal government. The committees found ways for the government to save billions of dollars, but most of their work was disregarded.

In 1962 the elderly president returned to Iowa to dedicate his Presidential Library at West Branch, where he had been born 88 years before. He died in New York two years later and was buried at West Branch.

The all-time record for U.S. Cabinet service belongs to an Iowan who was internationally renowned in his day, yet scarcely remembered now. James "Tama Jim" Wilson was born in Scotland but came to Tama County, Iowa, as a young man. Many of his contemporary politicians thought he might have become president if he had been native-born.

As head of agriculture at Iowa State University, as it is now called, he was a pioneer in studying and introducing scientific methods of agriculture.

For sixteen years he served as Secretary of Agriculture under McKinley, Roosevelt and Taft. His diplomatic and political skills in dealing with three such different executives amazed the nation. Throughout his career, Tama Jim was devoted to bringing modern methods to all farmers, worldwide. He was responsible for most of the techniques now used successfully to increase agricultural production.

"No other one person ever did so much to feed the world," according to one authority. Wilson insisted that all the discoveries should be shared to provide more food for more people worldwide. "He transformed the Department from a puny and almost disregarded arm of government into the strongest and farthest reaching of its kind on earth."

Another notable agricultural name belongs to three generations of the Wallace family. "Uncle Henry" Wallace was a pioneer in farm publication, as

THAT'S CURIOUS:
Tama Jim Wilson became Secretary of Agriculture at age 62, an age when most men are thinking of retiring. He did not retire until 78, still one of the dominant figures in government.

founder of "Wallace's Farmer." He did much to aid his friend Tama Jim Wilson in promoting scientific agriculture. His son, Henry C. Wallace, served as Secretary of Agriculture under Harding and Coolidge.

Grandson Henry A. Wallace (son of Henry C. Wallace) was one of the most controversial politicians of modern times. In early life he led in development of hybrid corn. Then he became F.D.R.'s Secretary of Agriculture.

In 1941 he became Roosevelt's vice president and was greatly disappointed to be replaced by Truman for the next term. If he had remained as vice president, he would have become president on Roosevelt's death.

Iowans have earned unusual distinction in the sciences outside of agriculture.

Dr. James Van Allen of the University of Iowa is the only modern person to have his name in the "heavens." The Van Allen belt of radiation patterns circling the earth was discovered through his efforts and named in his honor.

One of the nation's most distinguished black scientists received his major encouragement in Iowa.

A young Iowa State student named George Washington Carver was greatly assisted by Tama Jim Wilson at the college. Wilson called him "...by all means the ablest student we have here." Carver went on to become one of the leading scientific experimenters and educators of his day.

Iowa State University scientist Dr. W. Edwards Deming is credited with developing the first digital computer.

Iowa has produced some remarkable artists. Artist Grant Wood did most of his work in Iowa, using Iowa-related subjects. He quickly gained international fame and then lost favor for many years. A modern revival of interest has replaced him among the top American painters.

His painting of a dour-looking couple in front of a farmhouse has inspired hundreds of cartoons and jokes. This picture, "American Gothic," is one of the best known paintings of modern times.

One of the nation's best-recognized cartoonists was J.N. "Ding" Darling, who won a Pulitzer Prize for his work.

A Pulitzer Prize winning author was Margaret Wilson of Traer, for her fictional account of the Traer family called "The Able McLaughlins."

Writers Emerson Hough, Phil Stong, Ruth Suckow, MacKinlay Kantor, and James Norman Hall gained fame. The writer's workshop at the University of Iowa nurtured many highly lauded authors including James Michener, Kurt Vonnegut, Flannery O'Conner, and John Irving.

World-renowned composer Antonin Dvorak composed some interesting work at Spillville.

Meredith Willson, composer of "The Music Man," was a native of Mason City.

Iowa has developed a remarkable number of entertainers, including Johnny

THAT'S CURIOUS:
Antonin Dvorak used his shirt cuff to jot down notes for a sudden inspiration. He managed to rescue his shirt as it was about to go into the wash; from his notes came the "Indian Lament."

THAT'S CURIOUS:
An Iowan travelling in Scotland was so delighted with the famous Scottish oatmeal he ordered a barrel of it to be delivered to his home. When the barrel arrived from Scotland, it was labeled, "Quaker Oats, made in Cedar Rapids, Iowa."

Carson, John Wayne, Andy Williams, and Roger Williams, as well as a famed actress of an earlier period—Lillian Russell.

Two Iowa women were among the leaders in promoting women's rights. Voting rights advocate Carrie Chapman Catt lived at Charles City. Amelia Bloomer rebelled against the domination of men in many ways. One of these was her design of a "shocking" new costume, which came to be called bloomers in her honor.

One of the best-liked First Ladies was Mamie Eisenhower, a native of Boone.

A unique career was that of William F. Cody of Le Claire. He moved west and became the best-known of all the later frontiersmen. When he broke the record for killing buffalo, he became known as Buffalo Bill. Later he developed his Wild West and Rough Riders Show. With this he toured the world, even giving a performance for Queen Victoria, who loved his "bucking ponies." He went on to entertain other crowned heads all over Europe.

Buffalo Bill lost his fortune and died penniless, but his name lives on in legend.

A WEALTH OF NATURE

Of course, Iowa's rich soil is its greatest natural treasure. Protecting this soil from erosion and depletion is one of the state's top priorities. Most Iowa farmers are experts at the best methods of crop rotation, fertilization, contour plowing and other protective measures.

Other mineral wealth includes the large quantities of gypsum, mica, and coal.

Today the herds of wild buffalo are gone, but deer are so numerous as to cause problems in some areas. There are public hunting grounds for game and waterfowl. Scarce creatures are protected in wildlife refuges.

One of the most popular game birds, the pheasant, was imported a century ago from China, and hunters bag millions each year in the state.

USING THE WEALTH

Iowa is the world's preeminent food-producing area. Although more than 25 states are larger, Iowa grows more than 10 percent of the entire nation's production of food materials.

The state's farm income is well above ten billion dollars a year. The leader, California, is three times as large as Iowa but is not that far ahead in dollar value. Many of California's crops are specialty items, such as grapes for wine, and do not contribute to supplying urgent food needs.

Since 1952, for most years Iowa corn has been the largest single crop among the states in both number of bushels and dollar value. Much of the time Iowa leads in production of the invaluable soybean, oats and popcorn, dropping occasionally to second place.

Iowa gave birth to an important crop that is now mostly grown elsewhere.

When an apple tree was destroyed by lightning on Jesse Hiatt's farm near Peru, he carefully tended the new shoots. When they bore fruit, he noticed the apples were "deformed" with little nubs at the end, and he thought they were useless.

However, his friends said they were "delicious." We now know the fruit as the delicious apple, and every red delicious apple today is descended from that Iowa lightning bolt.

Iowa income from livestock tops all of the states, with world leadership in hog production, nearly equalling the total number of hogs of the next two states combined.

Flowers for seed and melons are among the leading specialty crops.

Summing up, Iowa boasts of the fact that each of its farmers produces enough to feed 279 people—three times the national average.

Naturally, Iowa manufacturing is much concerned with products and equipment relating to agriculture.

Charles W. Hart and Charles Parr of Charles City invented the word "tractor" to describe the machine they had produced, the first modern equipment of its type. Today, the John Deere tractor plant at Waterloo is the largest in the world.

The Quaker company at Cedar Rapids is one of the world's leading producers of a variety of grain products.

Many Iowa-manufactured products are known worldwide. The Sheaffer Pen Company at Fort Madison, the Maytag Company at Newton, the Lennox Company at Marshalltown, and the Amana Company in the Amanas have products with names recognized everywhere.

THE ECONOMY

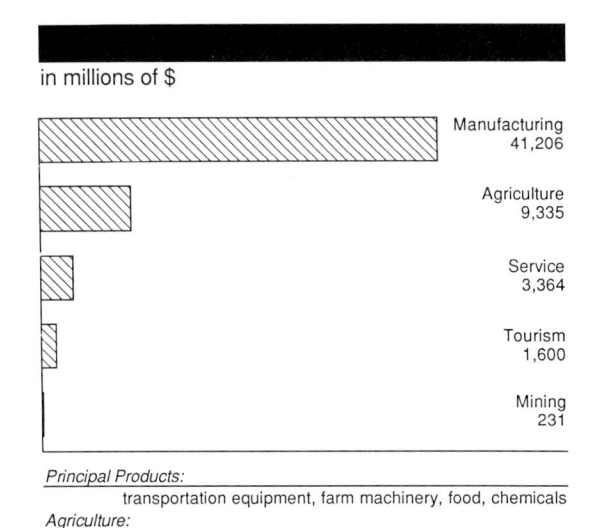

in millions of $

Manufacturing 41,206
Agriculture 9,335
Service 3,364
Tourism 1,600
Mining 231

Principal Products: transportation equipment, farm machinery, food, chemicals
Agriculture: corn, soybeans, hogs, cattle

The leading Iowa cities in industry are Cedar Rapids, Waterloo, Des Moines, and Dubuque.

The Cellophane plant at Clinton, and the aluminum plate rolling mill at Bettendorf are among the largest anywhere. A fourth of the Fortune 500 companies have operations in Iowa.

Insurance, publishing and printing are important. The Meredith Company of Des Moines is a leading producer of magazines and books.

GETTING AROUND

Dubuque is unlike other Iowa cities because of its picturesque location surmounting the bluffs of the Mississippi and looking down on that great river.

The view from Eagle Point Park is enhanced by the passage of boats and

Downtown Des Moines

barges through the Zebulon Pike locks, below.

As midwest cities go, Dubuque is an old city, but its historic houses give it an even older look. Some are open to the public as museums and restaurants.

An unusual treat for the midwest is the block-long cable car ride to the top of the lofty bluffs. Several paddle wheel steamers provide exciting river trips.

Another panorama of the Mississippi is had from McGregor Heights. Across the river, the great Wisconsin River empties into the Father of Waters.

Not far to the north of McGregor is Effigy Mounds National Monument.

Iowa's largest Mississippi River community is Davenport. Others are Clinton and Burlington.

Northwest of Davenport at West Branch is the Hoover Library, with its replica of the oval office, presidential papers and other mementoes of President and Mrs. Hoover. Their graves are nearby.

One of the most interesting of Iowa tourist attractions is the cluster of communities known as the Amana colonies. These seven villages with a large acreage of land were founded as a religious cooperative, where every person was equal in rights and responsibilities. It was perhaps the most successful of all the similarly organized groups.

No longer a cooperative, the Amana colonies still have wonderful restaurants with home cooking, wineries, handmade furniture and crafts, delightful inns, and attractive people. The Museum of Amana History gives a view of the colony's past.

THAT'S CURIOUS:
One of the most curious tourist attractions is the Squirrel Cage Jail at Council Bluffs. Inside the jail the cells are formed around a drum so that the jailer could have a continuous view of the prisoners, forming a kind of lazy susan.

The appliance products of Amana industries are known worldwide.

Nearby Cedar Rapids and Iowa City have many attractions.

One of the state's most attractive structures is the old capitol at Iowa City, now headquarters of the University of Iowa. That institution has been a leader in medicine, surgery, the teaching of writing, many fields of science, and other academic areas.

Waterloo, with adjoining Cedar Falls, is the metropolis of the northeast section.

Although Iowa has no huge cities, the capital and largest city, Des Moines, has many attractions. The dramatic capitol on its spacious grounds is outstanding of its type.

Des Moines has a fine collection of other museums, especially remarkable for a city of its size. These include the Art Center, Center of Science and Industry and the Botanical Center.

Particularly outstanding is Living History Farms near Des Moines. These fully operating farms include a farm of 1840, a horse farm of 1900, and a farm of today and tomorrow. There also is a reproduction of an 1870's community, called Walnut Hill.

The twin Iowa and Nebraska cities of Council Bluffs and Omaha form the metropolis of their section of the Missouri River.

Another Missouri River city is Sioux City, at the junction of the Big Sioux with the Missouri. Here is a monument to Sergeant Charles Floyd, of the Lewis and Clark expedition, who died there.

COMPAC-FACS
IOWA
The Hawkeye State

HISTORY
Statehood: December 18, 1846
Admitted as: 29th state
Capital: Des Moines, first settled 1843
OFFICIAL SYMBOLS
Motto: Our liberties we prize and our rights we will maintain
Bird: Eastern goldfinch
Flower: Wild rose
Tree: Oak
Song: "Song of Iowa"
Stone: Geode
GEO-FACS
Area: 56,275 sq. mi.
Rank in Area: 25th

Length (n/s): 209 mi.
Width (e/w): 301 mi.
Geographic Center: 5 mi. ne of Ames, Story County
Highest Point: 1,670 ft. (Sec. 29, T100N, R41W, Osceola County)
Lowest Point: 509 ft. (Mississippi River)
Mean Elevation: 1,100 ft.
Temperature, Extreme Range: 165 degrees
Number of Counties: 99

POPULATION
Total: 2,905,000 (1983)
Rank: 29th
Density: 52 persons per sq. mi.

The Iowa capitol gleams in the sun

Principal Cities: Des Moines, 191,003; Cedar Rapids, 110,243; Davenport, 103,264; Sioux City, 82,003; Waterloo, 75,985; Dubuque, 62,321; Council Bluffs, 56,449; Iowa City, 50,508; Ames, 45,775

EDUCATION
Schools: 2,055 elementary and secondary
Higher: 61

VITAL STATISTICS
Births (1980/83): 148,000
Deaths (1980/83): 88,000
Hospitals: 139
Drinking Age: 19

INTERESTING PEOPLE
Herbert Clark Hoover, James (Tama Jim) Wilson, Grant Wood, Dr. James van Allen, William F. (Buffalo Bill) Cody, Margaret Wilson, Jean Wilson Smith, Henry Wallace, Henry C. Wallace, Henry A. Wallace, Samuel Kirkwood, George Washington Carver, Dr. Norman Borlaug, Dr W. Edwards Deming, J.N. (Ding) Darling, Phil Stong, Ruth Suckow, MacKinlay Kantor, Emerson Hough, Meredith Willson, Johnny Carson, John Wayne, Andy Williams, Carrie Chapman Catt, Amelia Bloomer

WHEN DID IT HAPPEN?
1673: First exploration, Marquette and Jolliet
1762: Spanish acquire
1796: Julian Dubuque given land grant
1803: U.S. gains control
1804: Lewis and Clark explore; only death of expedition
1808: Fort Madison built
1833: Settlement becomes legal
1838: Iowa Territory formed
1846: Iowa becomes state
1854: The railroad arrives
1857: Capital moved to Des Moines
1867: Northwestern Railroad crosses state
1869: Iowa is a transcontinental railroad link
1877: Hog leadership first established
1913: Keokuk dam finished
1917: Iowans participate in World War I
1928: Herbert Hoover elected President
1952: Corn becomes first crop to earn a billion dollars
1963: Atomic research reactor started at Ames
1976: Democrats control Legislature
1985: Farm crisis deepens

MICHIGAN

FASCINATING MICHIGAN

Michigan is a state where a major city was given its name because two ladies sat under a grapevine. It is the land where the snowshoe and birchbark canoe were invented, a land claimed in a unique ceremony.

Michigan has unique distinction in its merchant princes and industrial giants; it is the home of breakfast food, and the birthplace of a president who assumed the presidency under the most unusual circumstances in presidential history.

A Michigan man made medical history because of a "window" in his stomach; another was crowned America's first and only "King."

Michigan is a state with the courage to choose a "wilderness" as a capital and to select the youngest governor in the country's history.

These lively and interesting facts help to illuminate the life and times of one of the nation's greatest recreational and industrial giants.

THE FACE OF MICHIGAN

Nearly half of the state of Michigan is water, 40 percent to be exact. No other area of its size can boast such a proportion of fresh water—one of the world's greatest treasures.

If the water area of 40,032 square miles is added to the land—56,954 square miles—Michigan is the largest state east of the Mississippi River.

Most of this water area comes from the parts of the four Great Lakes within Michigan's borders.

Thaquamenon Falls

The name of the state itself reflects this abundance of water. In the Indian language "michi" means large. "Gama" is the Indian word for lake, so the name literally means "great lake." It has 11,000 beautiful inland lakes.

Michigan's most important "rivers" are really not rivers at all. The St. Clair, Detroit, and St. Mary's rivers are actually straits, connecting bodies of water.

Cut into two distinct parts, upper and lower, Michigan is the only state with such a separation.

Michigan's unusual borders provide some unexpected facts of geography. At Port Huron, Michigan extends as far east as parts of South Carolina, an Atlantic state. The distance from Detroit to Baltimore, Maryland, is less than the distance within Michigan from Houghton to Detroit.

55

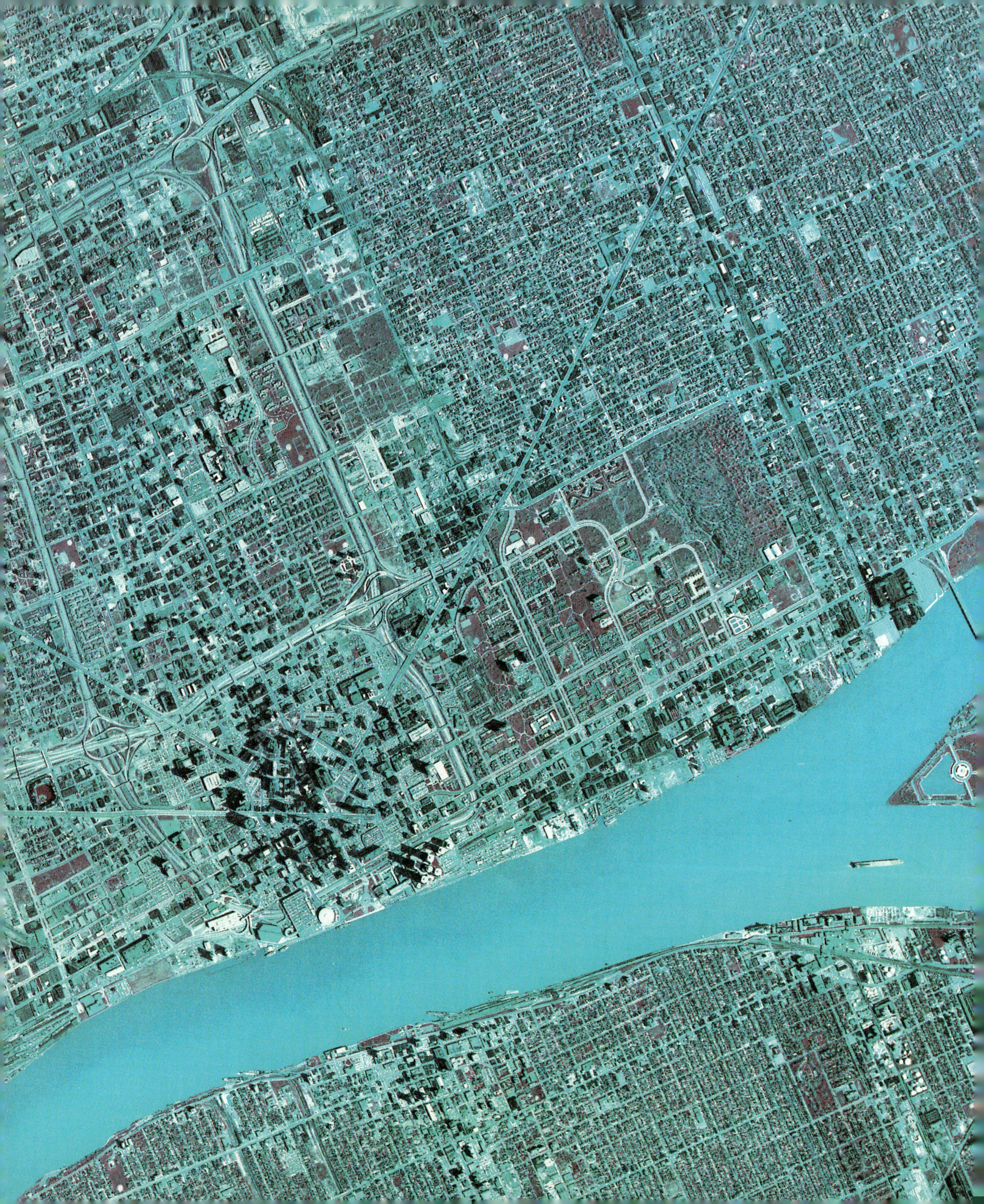

THAT'S CURIOUS:
Even though Michigan is an "inland" state, its shoreline of 3,177 miles is second only to mighty Alaska's. Before Alaska became a state, Michigan had the longest shoreline of all.

In another twist of geography, a good part of the "northern" neighbor, Canada, lies south of Michigan.

Michigan must have been a land of water in ancient times, also. Several times the land level lowered and shallow seas swept in over a period of millenia.

Frozen water also played its part in shaping the state. Much of the present topography of Michigan is due to the forces and weight of the four glaciers which pushed across the present area.

One of the most interesting geographic features of the state is the high border of sand which extends along the Lake Michigan shoreline. Some of these sand dunes are among the largest anywhere.

Isle Royale, Mackinac Island, Beaver Island and the Manitou Islands are the principal offshore portions of the state.

EARLY DWELLERS

Remote Isle Royale has some of the most interesting reminders of the prehistoric peoples who lived in what is now Michigan. Those people worked more than 10,000 small copper mining pits. They may have done skillful copper work at the time of early Egyptian civilization.

As a whole, Michigan has fewer relics of ancient civilizations than nearby states. There are some burial mounds, a few weapons and various implements to give some indication of how the prehistoric people lived.

When the Indians of the area first became known to history, they had apparently lost the metal working and many other skills of the people who may have been their ancestors. The native people in the 17th century were using only stone implements. European explorers found a number of tribes including the Chippewa, Potawatomi, Ottawa, Miami and Menominee. Later, groups of the Huron came in.

As time went by, most of the settled tribes were driven out of the lower peninsula by the Iroquois from the east.

Europeans quickly adopted many Indian ways. Principal of these were the snowshoe and the birchbark canoe. The snowshoe was essential for overland travel in the bitter winters. The birchbark canoe was probably the lightest and most practical of all small craft.

STIRRINGS

Etienne Brule is thought to have been the first European to reach present Michigan, not later than 1622 and perhaps as early as 1618.

Missionaries, fur traders, trappers, and other explorers followed.

By 1668 a French settlement had been made at Sault Sainte Marie by the missionary-explorer Father Jacques Marquette.

Three years later, a strange ceremony took place at the Sault (called Soo). A crowd of Indians was seated on the river banks. They had been told that there would be wonderful events.

When the mission doors opened, a group of missionaries came out in a

(Opposite) Detroit as viewed from on high

procession followed by a man dressed in the splendid uniform of a French officer. Hunters, trappers, interpreters and other attendants joined the procession, all adorned with gaudy accessories to impress the Indians.

A large wooden cross was raised, and the officer proclaimed possession of all the lands to the west, north, and south. Shots were fired and "long live the King," resounded three times. The Indians were told of his majesty's greatness, and they were awed. This event has come to be known as the Pageant of the Sault.

The "coureurs de bois" (trappers) and "voyageurs" (boatmen) continued to operate in the region, but comparatively few settlers came. All of French Canada had only about 20,000 permanent European residents in 1689, compared to 300,000 English on the east coast.

To counter the growing British threat, the French began to build forts. The explorer La Salle erected lower Michigan's first French fort in 1679, at what is now St. Joseph.

EARLY GROWTH

In 1701 a French town was founded on the land between Lake Erie and Lake Huron. Because it was on a strait, the community was called Detroit, which means "on a strait" in French. This tiny beginning was the start of the first major city of the midwest.

The name of the founder of Detroit is now a famous name, but only because it is seen almost everywhere every day on the luxury automobile that bears his name. He was Antoine de la Mothe Cadillac.

The year 1715 saw another French stronghold set up—Fort Michilimackinac on the Straits of Mackinac.

Periods of war and peace followed. Then Major Robert Rogers brought two hundred Royal English Rangers and captured Detroit in 1760.

The French had treated the Indians well, but the British scorned them. This brought almost immediate trouble. Chief Pontiac laid siege to Detroit in 1763. After the longest siege in the history of Indian warfare, Pontiac finally gave up. The siege had lasted 175 days.

However, Detroit was the only fort in Michigan that did not fall to the Indians, giving them their greatest of all successes in the struggle to put out the Europeans.

Pontiac's victories could not last long, and he was brought to the peace table.

The French had already given up their hold on the North American continent; now it appeared it might be the British turn, when the American Revolution began.

The story of the Revolution in the "back country" beyond the Atlantic Coast is not so well known, but it was critical in saving the vast region for the future United States.

The Americans were not able to capture Detroit, which was under the control of the hated British Governor Henry Hamilton. He was known as the Hair Buyer because he paid the Indians money to bring the scalps of Americans.

At the end of the Revolution, the

THAT'S CURIOUS:
La Salle built the first European-style boat on the Great Lakes, and named it the "Griffon." It set sail with a load of furs and no one ever knew what became of it.

Early Detroit, painting by A. C. Warren

British agreed to give up Michigan and the other western regions, but they hung on in some areas for another 13 years.

A famous Revolutionary General "Mad" Anthony Wayne came into the region, defeated the Indians and marched into Detroit in 1796. He was given a wild welcome, and several towns and institutions in Michigan have taken his name, including a university, a fort, a museum, a city and a county.

TERRITORIES

Michigan became part of the vast region known as the Northwest Territory. The parts of this region were to be given the opportunity to become states as soon as their populations were large enough.

In 1805 Michigan Territory was created from the larger area. In that same year Detroit was almost completely destroyed by fire. The city was rebuilt on a much grander plan.

When another war with Britain began in 1812, most of Michigan was soon surrendered to the British. There were Indian massacres, such as at Raisin River, and many hardships. The people of Detroit had a difficult time during the

THAT'S CURIOUS:
The Indians stole the organ pipes from Father Gabriel Richard's church in Detroit. When he let it be known that these were the flutes of the Great Spirit, this powerful "magic" was returned and replaced.

59

British occupation. The thievery of the Indians was especially hard to take.

After the British fleet was beaten on Lake Erie, the Americans were able to take Detroit. In September, 1813, just before American General Duncan McArthur marched in, the British burned the public buildings and left.

Territorial Governor Lewis Cass served for a long period, from 1813 to 1831. In 1820 he set out by canoe on a famous 4,000-mile survey of the territory. He and his party calmed the Indians and discovered many rich resources of the area. This helped to attract settlers.

When the Erie Canal opened in New York, in 1825, people had an easier water route to Detroit and other parts of Michigan; larger numbers of settlers and business people poured in.

In 1831 Stevens T. Mason had been appointed Secretary of the Territory. He became acting governor at the age of nineteen, probably the youngest person to hold such an office in the history of the country. He was noted for his capable administrations.

In the decade of 1830 to 1840, almost 200,000 people came to Michigan.

STATEHOOD

Michigan qualified as a state when, in 1835, the people of Michigan approved a constitution and elected officers. They chose Stevens T. Mason, then twenty-four, as governor.

However, there were border problems, and Congress refused to recognize the new state. Michigan claimed its borders included the part of Lake Erie occupied by the city of Toledo. Ohio disputed this.

Finally Michigan gave up the claim and exchanged this small area for the vast Upper Peninsula. Some thought this was not a very good deal, but of course it proved to have enormous advantages.

Still, Congress was reluctant to admit another free state. At last, when Arkansas was ready as a slave state, Congress gave in, and Michigan became the 26th state in January, 1837.

Three years later, Dr. Douglass Houghton made a discovery which showed the value of the Upper Peninsula. He had found the important copper deposits there.

Detroit had remained the capital city, but the legislature wanted a more central location. When they could not agree on an established town, they chose a location with one log house and a sawmill. This was Lansing.

In January of 1848, the seat of government was moved to this "Capital in the Wilderness."

A MODERN STATE

In the growing disagreement over slavery, most Michigan people were strongly opposed to "ownership" of human beings. A group of them met in a "Convention Under the Oaks" on July 6, 1854. They formed a Republican Party. Several states claim the honor of the party's origin, but Michigan's claim is perhaps the best. In the election that year, Michigan was the first state to choose a Republican as a governor.

THAT'S CURIOUS:
Beginning in 1849, Beaver Island was ruled by a "King." James Jesse Strang led a group of Mormon settlers there. He had his followers proclaim him King, and ruled as an absolute monarch. However, mainland mobs assassinated Strang in 1856, and the kingdom ended.

Artist Robert Thom recreates the fight of Michigan's 24th regiment at Gettysburg. ©1967 Michigan Bell Telephone Co.

When the Civil War came, Michigan troops played an important part throughout the conflict. Their bravery was particularly important in the battles at Chattanooga and Gettysburg. As the war came to an end, Michigan troops discovered and captured Jefferson Davis, Confederate president.

A terrible forest fire swept through a wide area from border to border, destroying Holland and much of Manistee, leaving 18,000 people homeless.

This great fire did not get much international attention because in a sadly strange coincidence it began on October 8, 1871, the same day Chicago was destroyed by fire. Many of Chicago's wooden structures had been built of Michigan timbers.

The labor movement was popular in Michigan. In 1885 the working people won a particularly significant victory. A new law declared ten hours was a legal working day. Some laborers had been required to work as many as 18 hours a day.

As a new century began, the infant auto industry took hold in Detroit and began a rapid growth which made Michigan the center of world automobile manufacturing.

Throughout World War I, Michigan's manufacturing skills and the ability of Michigan soldiers played a key role.

During the depression, beginning in 1929, few people could afford automobiles, so times in Michigan were particularly difficult.

The expertise of Michigan's factories was an essential part of victory in World

PEOPLES

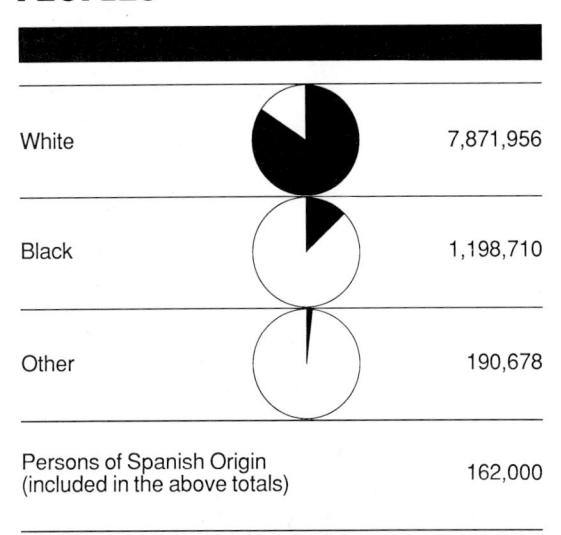

White		7,871,956
Black		1,198,710
Other		190,678
Persons of Spanish Origin (included in the above totals)		162,000

War II. More than an eighth of the entire production of war supplies came from the state during the war. The incredible output of a B-24 bomber every hour was produced by Ford at Willow Run. The Defoe Company was able to turn out a new fighting boat every week.

A glider contributed by the children of Michigan was the first to land on a Normandy beach during D-Day.

During the Korean War the first American troops to see action were the forces of the Michigan National Guard.

One of the great man-made wonders was completed in 1957. For the first time the upper and lower portions of the state were linked by a bridge over the Straits of Mackinac. This wonderful span has become known as "Big Mac."

During the general period of racial unrest in the 1960's, a large section of Detroit was destroyed in the 1967 riots.

A great effort has been made to keep downtown Detroit important. The 1970's saw the opening of a splendid downtown complex called the Renaissance Center.

Due to the ups and downs of the auto industry and the competition from Japanese automakers, Michigan has had some difficult times in recent years.

By 1985 the auto industry seemed to have regained much of its market, but there was no assurance it would continue.

PERSONALITIES

Michigan has produced only one American President. Gerald R. Ford has been the only chief executive in the nation's history to become president without being elected either as president or vice president.

When Vice President Spiro Agnew resigned, Ford was appointed to fill the post. He had been a leading congressman for many years. Upon the resignation of President Richard Nixon, Gerald Ford became president.

Ford proved to be an outstanding administrator. However, many voters resented his pardon of President Nixon, and he was not reelected.

A two-time but unsuccessful candidate for president was Thomas E. Dewey, native of Owosso. National fame came to him when he was Governor of New York.

One of the best-known names in American history is that of General George Armstrong Custer. As one of the youngest Union generals, he became a Civil War hero. Later Custer led his men into the Battle of Little Big Horn, where he and all his men were massacred by the Indians in one of the nation's worst defeats. There is much controversy about General Custer's part, but it is now thought that he acted unwisely and probably brought on the defeat.

By contrast, peace was the quest of Ralph J. Bunche, Detroit native who was the U.S. Representative in the United Nations. He won the Nobel Peace Prize in 1950.

Another noble man of peace was Father Gabriel Richard, sometimes known as "The Patron Saint of Detroit." This remarkable man had a leading role in almost every civic effort in Michigan. He printed the first Michigan book and published the first newspaper, helped to found the University of Michigan, was a territorial representative to the U.S. Congress and took extraordinary care of his parishioners.

During the terrible cholera epidemic at Detroit, Father Richard was tireless in helping the sick and finally died of the disease. There were more people in attendance at his funeral than the total population of Detroit at the time.

Few people have had the worldwide influence of Michigan's Henry Ford. Ford made two giant contributions to 20th-century life, and had an outstanding failure which added almost as much to his international fame.

Ford knew that if automobiles could be made cheaply enough in large numbers, most Americans could have a car. He created ways of making cars on assembly lines which brought the price down. He also believed that if workers were treated fairly they would produce more and better work.

Ford Motor Company commissioned artist Norman Rockwell to paint Henry Ford at work

In 1914 Henry Ford promised his workers the then unheard-of sum of $5.00 for an eight-hour day. Ford proved he could pay higher wages and still make a profit. The idea of a car in every American garage took off.

While World War I was raging in Europe, Ford decided he could help by calling a peace conference and sending the Ford Peace Ship to Europe. Nothing came of this, but because of this gesture he received great attention.

THAT'S CURIOUS:
Alexis St. Martin suffered an abdominal gunshot wound that never healed, but he recovered and seemed healthy. Dr. William Beaumont observed the digestive processes through this "window in the stomach." His observations on digestion have proved useful ever since. St. Martin lived to be 80 years old.

Before his death, Henry Ford worked with his son Edsel to create the Ford Foundation, one of the largest of all. This was to help improve education, culture, government and public affairs.

Michigan seems to have an unusual distinction as home of "merchant princes." Aaron Montgomery Ward spent his boyhood in Niles and pioneered in the huge mail-order firm that bears his name. Sebastian S. Kresge, Detroit, founded a variety store chain that has grown to be one of the world's largest merchandising organizations. Joseph L. Hudson founded the large department store chain that bears his name. Harry Gordon Selfridge began his career at Jackson and went on to become one of England's leading merchants.

A WEALTH OF NATURE

The copper boulder found at Ontonagon was the largest ever seen. It emphasized the value of the state's copper deposits. Michigan's reserves of coal and peat provide other substantial mineral resources. While much of the state's best iron has been mined, lower-grade ores still remain.

The most obvious natural treasures were the great forests, with 85 varieties of trees. Much of the state's wealth was based on this resource.

The forests have been home to a wide variety of animals, including the wolverine. Though Michigan is the Wolverine State, few if any have been seen in recent times.

Until 1912, moose had not been known on Isle Royale. They were able to cross over on the ice in that year, the nucleus of the island's present herd.

USING THE WEALTH

From 1840 to 1900 Michigan was the principal lumbering state. In that time enough wood came from the state to cover it with an inch-thick floor of wood. Trees were called green gold, and they brought in more wealth than even the real gold of California.

When the forests were worked out, lumbering declined, but modern replanting and new methods have restored much pulp, paper, veneer and saw timber activity.

At one time Michigan was the leading copper state and one of the leaders in iron mining. Those minerals are still important. Processing of iron and steel began in Michigan in 1864.

Perhaps unexpectedly, Michigan leads the nation in salt production. The state's leading chemical companies depend on salt brines for much of their operations.

Oil and gas reserves are still being discovered and developed in the state.

In agriculture, Michigan is known for its plentiful red cherries and other specialty crops such as mints of various kinds and navy beans.

Almost 2,500 different manufactured products are made in Michigan. However, most famous of all are automobiles, breakfast foods, and furniture.

The breakfast flakes and other cereals so popular today originated with two men, W.K. Kellogg and C.W. Post. The businesses they established at Battle Creek dominate the prepared breakfast food market.

The hardwood forests of Michigan provide the materials for the furniture industry, centered at Grand Rapids.

One of the largest cement plants in

the world is located at Alpena. Presque Isle's limestone quarry has been called "the largest in the world." Grindstone City takes its name from the sharpening equipment it turned out in such quantities that at one time it almost had a monopoly on grindstones.

In spite of foreign competition and many present problems, the American automobile industry has made a substantial comeback, and its center is still in Michigan, particularly Detroit and the surrounding areas. The city "remade America with the automobile and then remade the world with the techniques they have learned in the automobile plants."

Michigan steam autos first appeared in 1884. Detroit did not see a gasoline engine car until Charles G. King built one in 1896. In 1900 Henry Ford thrilled the city with his first car. "The machine runs, stops and backs at his will. He turns sharp curves with the grace and ease of a wild bird under full sail," a local newspaper reported.

By 1904 Ransom E. Olds had turned out 5,000 "Oldsmobiles" in Lansing. The Model T was first introduced by Ford in 1908. That same year saw the General Motors company organized. The last of the "Big Three" automakers was formed in 1925, when Walter P. Chrysler organized his company.

Today more than three fourths of all American-made automobiles are products of Michigan auto corporations.

Other forms of transportation are important to Michigan, particularly on the Great Lakes on which the state has so many borders.

The Soo Canal is probably the busiest in the world. The earliest canal was finished in 1855, and the canals and locks have been expanded several times. The Detroit River holds first place in water-borne tonnage.

The 1959 opening of the St. Lawrence Seaway gave Michigan ports direct access to the sea.

The first regularly scheduled passenger air service in the U.S. was commenced in 1926 between Grand Rapids and Detroit.

THE ECONOMY

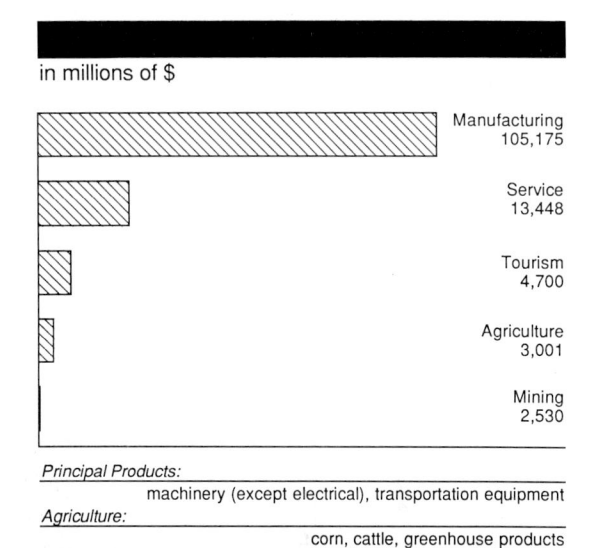

in millions of $

Manufacturing	105,175
Service	13,448
Tourism	4,700
Agriculture	3,001
Mining	2,530

Principal Products: machinery (except electrical), transportation equipment
Agriculture: corn, cattle, greenhouse products

GETTING AROUND

The enormous frontage of Michigan on the Great Lakes and the hundreds of beautiful interior lakes of the state truly create a "Water Wonderland." Almost every type of water recreation can be found in Michigan.

Just back from the Lake Michigan shores another unusual recreational opportunity stretches near the shore for

The Ford Museum at Dearborn features a replica of Independence Hall

several hundred miles. The great lakeshore dunes provide a unique and special kind of recreation, with their natural attractions, dune buggies, sand skiing and other delights.

A particularly attractive tourist area is the northernmost part of the lower peninsula. Fort Michilimacknac has been rebuilt; it lies in the shadow of the great suspension bridge, a man made beauty in itself. Nearby Traverse City is home of the annual Cherry Festival.

One of the country's most unusual island-retreats brings scores of tourists to Mackinac Island. The world's largest summer hotel, old Fort Mackinac, scores of shops, and restaurants all add to the attraction.

Particularly interesting is the absence of automobile traffic on Mackinac Island. Motor vehicles are forbidden.

On Beaver Island twenty buildings of the period of the "King" of the Island, James J. Strang, have been opened to the public.

Far to the north is Michigan's only National Park, Isle Royale. With no roads or wheeled vehicles the entire large island is almost completely in its natural state. This is true of much of the Upper Peninsula.

One of the top tourist attractions is the region of Sault Sainte Marie, Michigan's oldest city, with the St. Mary's River and the canals and locks.

Winter skiing is another favorite pastime of the Upper Peninsula.

Perhaps the most popular single tourist attraction in Michigan is Henry Ford Museum and Greenfield Village, Dearborn, just to the west of Detroit.

Henry Ford established this complex to pay particular tribute to past life in America and especially to emphasize the importance of invention and industry. More than 100 historic buildings have been moved to Greenfield Village, including Ford's own birthplace. The Wright bicycle shop was moved there to show the locale where the airplane originated. Thomas Edison's laboratory at Menlo Park, New Jersey, has been completely reproduced.

The vast museum has one of the largest displays of transportation equipment, as well as many other types of display.

At Dearborn Inn, visitors can stay overnight in the historic homes of such famous men and women as Edgar Allan Poe or Barbara Fritchie.

Also at Dearborn is perhaps the

largest non-governmental manufacturing establishment in the world—Ford's River Rouge plant.

Detroit is the oldest major city in the Midwest. The Veterans' Memorial building now stands on the site where Cadillac founded the community.

This is part of the impressive Civic Center, where the 1955 City-County Building also rises.

Among the principal Detroit attractions is its accessibility to another nation and another culture, with Canada just on the other side of the Detroit River, by bridge or tunnel.

Belle Island Park in the river provides a zoo, aquarium, horseback riding and other attractions.

While the Renaissance Center has had its trouble in attracting visitors and tenants, it is still an outstanding showpiece of its type. The towering hotel at the heart of the center is impressive.

The Gerald Ford Library is located at Lansing.

The great capitol at Lansing was constructed from the local sandstone. A rotunda looking up 175 feet to the dome is encompassed by two grand staircases. The Civil War battle flags have been a popular feature.

For its era (1879) the capitol was much ahead of its time. It was one of the first major buildings to be lighted with gas lamps activated with electric switches. Its steam-powered elevator was a wonder of its period.

Michigan State Police Headquarters at Lansing is noted worldwide for the nation's second largest collection of fingerprints.

Grand Rapids is the second largest city in the state. Not surprisingly, the Public Museum features its furniture collection.

The Gerald Ford Museum at Grand Rapids honors the state's only native president.

During the tulip season, it would appear that most of the country is making trek to Holland's annual festival. Dutch costumes, parades, pageants and the universal flood of tulip blossoms are among the features.

Holland is home to considerable manufacturing, including the nation's only wooden-shoe producer.

COMPAC-FACS

MICHIGAN
The Wolverine State - The Great Lake State
Water Wonderland

HISTORY
Statehood: January 26, 1837
Admitted as: 26th state
Capital: Lansing, founded 1847
OFFICIAL SYMBOLS
Motto: Si Quaeris Peninsulam Amoenam, Circumspice ("If You Seek a Pleasant Peninsula, Look Around You")
Bird: Robin
Fish: Brook trout
Flower: Apple blossom
Tree: White pine
Song: "Michigan, My Michigan"
Gem: Isle Royal greenstone (Chlorastrolite)
GEO-FACS
Area: 56,954 sq. mi.
Rank in Area: 23rd (land only)

THAT'S CURIOUS:

Ann Arbor got its name because two husbands watched their wives chatting under their grape arbor. The women were both named Ann, so the husbands gave the town its name. Ann Arbor boasts one of the major centers of learning—the University of Michigan.

The Michigan capitol

Length (n/s): 286 mi. (Upper Peninsula)
Width (e/w): 400 mi.
Geographic Center: South section of Worcester, Worcester County
Highest Point: 1,979 (Mt. Arvon)
Lowest Point: 572 ft. (Lake Erie)
Mean Elevation: 900 ft.
Temperature, Extreme Range: 163 degrees
Number of Counties: 83
Water Area: 40,032 sq. mi. (total within boundaries)
Shoreline: 3,177 mi.
POPULATION
Total: 9,069,000 (1983)
Rank: 8th
Density: 159 persons per sq. mi.
Principal Cities: Detroit, 1,203,339; Grand Rapids, 181,843; Warren, 161,134; Flint, 159,611; Lansing, 130,414; Sterling Heights, 108,999; Ann Arbor, 107,966
EDUCATION
Schools: 4,544 (elementary and secondary)
Higher: 93

VITAL STATISTICS
Births (1980/83): 457,000
Deaths (1980/83): 248,000
Hospitals: 233
Drinking Age: 21
INTERESTING PEOPLE
Gerald R. Ford, George Armstrong Custer, Thomas Dewey, Henry Ford, Edgar Guest, Walter P. Chrysler, Ralph Bunche, Father Gabriel Richard, Diana Ross, Stevie Wonder, Antoine de la Mothe Cadillac, S.S. Kresge, J.L. Hudson, A. Montgomery Ward, Ransom E. Olds, C.W. Post, W. K. Kellogg, Sebastian Kresge
WHEN DID IT HAPPEN?
1618: First known Europeans
1634: Nicolet at Straits of Mackinac
1668: Sault Sainte Marie founded by Marquette and Dablon
1671: Daumont claims for France
1701: Detroit founded by Cadillac
1760: French forced from Detroit
1783: Treaty of Paris seals America's claim
1787: Northwest Ordinance provides government
1805: Michigan Territory created
1812: Detroit taken by British
1818: First steamboat
1835: Border dispute with Ohio settled
1837: Statehood
1847: Lansing is capital
1854: Republican Party founded
1871: Fires sweep state
1879: Capitol dedicated
1908: First Model T Ford
1929: Ambassador Bridge in use to Canada
1935: United Automobile Workers founded
1957: Mackinac Bridge dedicated
1959: St. Lawrence Seaway provides outlet to sea
1974: Gerald R. Ford assumes presidency
1977: Detroit Renaissance Center dedicated
1985: Auto industry prospers

MINNESOTA

FASCINATING MINNESOTA

Typical of the modesty of the people, Minnesota boasts of only 10,000 lakes, which leaves about 5,000 left over.

There is, of course, much to boast about in the North Star State, as well as many facts and incidents that make its story lively and interesting.

These include the great city once known as Pig's Eye and the pig that made a great discovery.

Among the Minnesotans of widespread reputation are the nine-year-old anaesthetist and the mining tycoon who named a rich claim after his dog.

Over the years a major Minnesota waterfall "traveled" more than four miles.

Minnesota history includes the incidents of the Cow War and the war that featured a stovepipe cannon, as well as the fright of the Indians when the snorting monster came to visit.

Perhaps most significant is the beautiful red stone found only in Minnesota which came to symbolize peace throughout the native population.

THE FACE OF MINNESOTA

The objective of one of the greatest searches in geography was finally found in what is now Minnesota.

"What had long been sought at last appeared suddenly...the cheering sight of a transparent body of water burst upon our view." That was the way explorer Henry R. Schoolcraft described his 1832 discovery of the source of the Mississippi River, the small lake called Itasca.

Minnesota is not only the source of the Mississippi, but the St. Louis River is also considered to be the source of the system that drains the Great Lakes by way of the distant St. Lawrence River.

The state's rivers flow not only south and east but also north, separated by three distinct watersheds or divides. The mighty Red River of the North begins at the junction of the Bois de Sioux and Otter Tail rivers at Breckenridge. The Red makes its way along the Minnesota-North Dakota border and finally empties into remote Hudson Bay.

In total, Minnesota contains 25,000 miles of rivers and streams, including the St. Croix and Red Lake River.

Not surprisingly, however, the state is even more famous as Land of 10,000 Lakes. Actually there are more than 15,000 according to later counts. There are so many lakes that a number of them have the same name. There are 91 Long Lakes and many other duplications.

Minnesota boundaries include 2,212 square miles of clear, deep Lake Superior. The largest lake entirely within the state is Red Lake, covering 440 square miles. Larger Lake of the Woods is shared with Canada.

THAT'S CURIOUS:
An unusual feature of Minnesota is the traveling falls. Waters of St. Anthony's Falls carved so deeply into the soft limestone that the falls have moved upriver almost four miles since discovery.

69

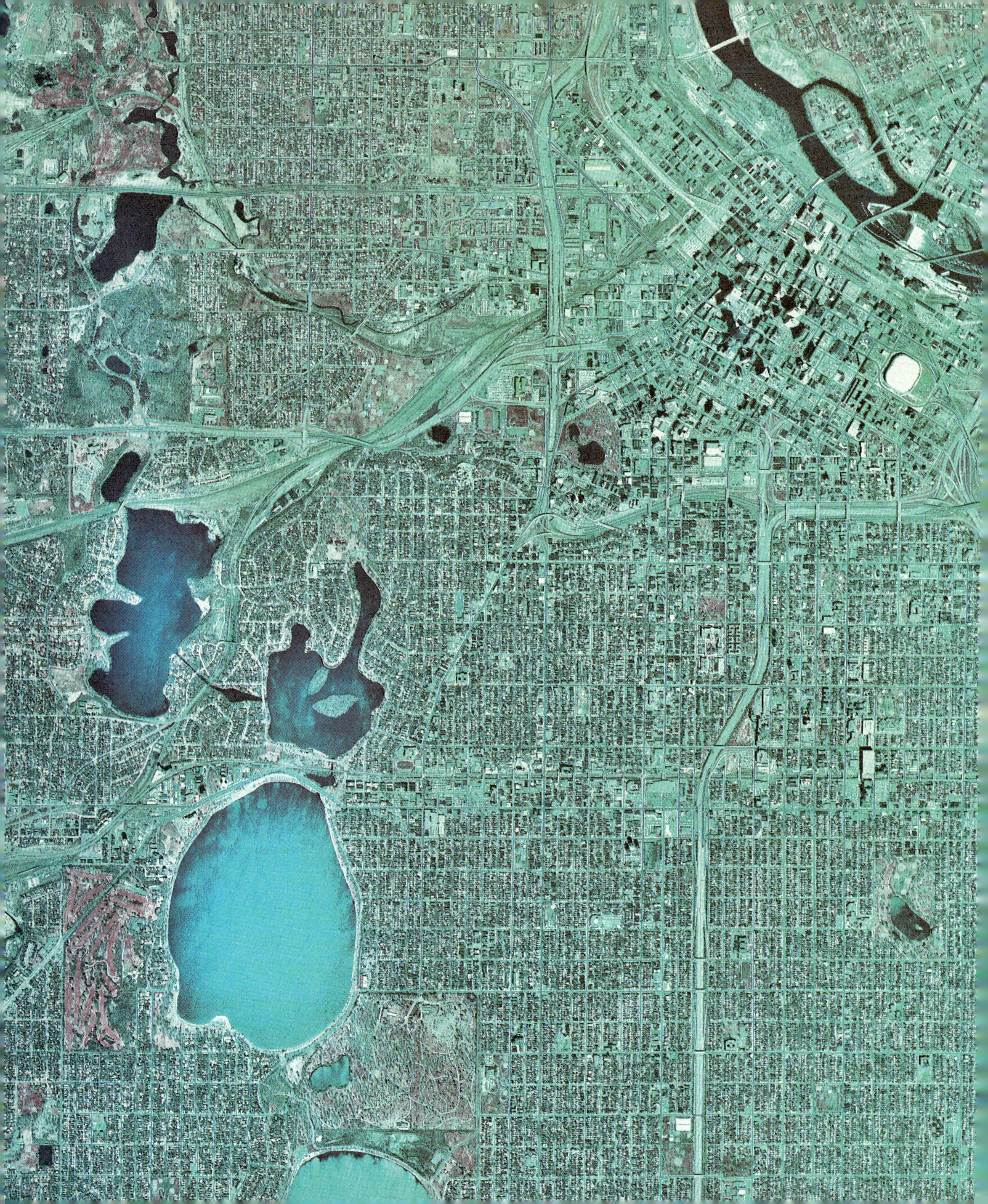

Lake Pepin straddles the Mississippi River and is formed by a natural dam across the river. This was formed by the debris brought in from Wisconsin's Chippewa River.

It is hard to believe that this quiet, generally level land once had giant mountains and fiery volcanoes. Ancient mountains were leveled and seas rolled in several times over millions of years.

Four different times the present state was almost entirely covered by the glaciers. They filled in some valleys, carved new ones, brought soil and boulders from distant areas, piled up high ridges and left the land vastly changed.

As the glaciers melted they left huge ancient lakes now called Lake Agassiz, Lake Aitkin and Lake Duluth. Lake Superior is what is left of the latter.

Not all of the rich soil was brought by the glaciers. The loess soil of the southeast was deposited by winds.

The point of land known as the Chimney is the northernmost point of the 48 conterminous states. Because of the Lake of the Woods, the Chimney cannot be reached by land except through Canada.

EARLY DWELLERS

Some very important finds in archeology have been made in Minnesota.

A teenage drowning victim may have lived near present Pelican Rapids as long ago as 20,000 years. This discovery was called Minnesota Man. Because the skeleton was that of a female, laymen call it the Lady of the Lake.

Near Browns Valley another important skeleton was unearthed and called Browns Valley Man. It was thought to be around 12,000 years old.

The mighty Mississippi has small beginnings; (Opposite) Minneapolis as seen by NHAP/EROS

More than 10,000 prehistoric mounds, village sites, stone dams, drawings and paintings are among the other relics of ancient peoples in the area.

Dacotah Indians, a branch of the Sioux nation, were the first Indian group mentioned in historical records. The Ojibwa Indians, called Chippewa, were an Algonquin group pushed westward by eastern settlement and pressure of stronger tribes. In turn they were able to drive the Sioux people westward because they had guns obtained in the East.

The Sioux were people of the plains and the Chippewa forest dwellers.

The Sioux made a wonderfully nourishing pressed meat called pemmican. They especially enjoyed buffalo tongue and the meat from the buffalo hump behind the shoulders.

71

Famed artist of Indian life, George Catlin, painted this scene of the Sioux gathering wild rice

Blueberries were dried and stored for food.

Wild rice was a necessity. The Indian women would push through the marshes where the rice grows, pulling the grains into their canoes. The wild rice is still reserved to the Indians.

The only physical work done by the Indian men was stomping the rice grain to separate it from the chaff. Warfare and hunting were the other male duties.

The Chippewa tapped the hard maple trees and boiled down the syrup for maple sugar. They lived in wigwams made of poles covered by birchbark. The same bark provided their wonderfully light canoes.

The Sioux used a clumsy kind of boat of buffalo skins, and pulled heavy loads on a sled called a travois, hitched to a horse.

One of the unusual features of Minnesota is the pipestone, found only in the area. The pipestone quarries were sacred places to the Indians; all could go there in peace to chop out pieces of the dark red rock from which peace pipes were carved.

The pipes were passed around a circle of men as a symbol of peace. Before tobacco was known, dried dogwood leaves were smoked.

Minnesota Indians became well known and popular through such writings as Longfellow's "The Song of Hiawatha."

STIRRINGS

Did Norse explorers reach Minnesota as early as 1362, more than 100 years before Columbus sailed?

This is the story told on a famous

carved stone found by Olaf Ohman on his farm near Kensington. Its inscriptions appeared to be done in a carved writing known as runes. Some authorities believe this Kensington runestone is a true relic, while others call it a hoax.

However, many signs indicate the runestone may be authentic. Tree roots had grown around it, showing at least 70 years of age. The stone was done with expert skill. Who would have been interested in planting a hoax at such an early time? Also, Norwegian implements of the 1300's have been found in Minnesota.

The mystery may never be solved.

First-known European visitor to Minnesota was Daniel Greysolon, known as Sieur du Lhut, or Duluth.

Explorers Father Louis Hennepin, Accault and Du Gay were taken prisoner by the Indians and forced to travel across much of the present state. These 1680 prisoners were the first Europeans known to have visited the Minneapolis/St.Paul region.

Duluth heard of the prisoners and persuaded the Indians to release them.

To get from French Canada to Minnesota, French travelers established three main routes. One of the three principal routes into Minnesota was pioneered by La Verendrye, a noble Frenchman, with his sons and nephew. They traversed the canoe route from Lake Superior to Lake Winnipeg. Probably this group represented the first Europeans to reach the Red River Valley.

The Red River and Red Lake route became another of the principal routes in Minnesota.

The route from Green Bay and down the Wisconsin River was the other main passage to reach the Minnesota region from French Canada.

Because the Indians wanted the mirrors, blankets, knives, and other European products, French traders called "voyageurs" found their way into almost every part of present Minnesota. The items were exchanged for valuable furs.

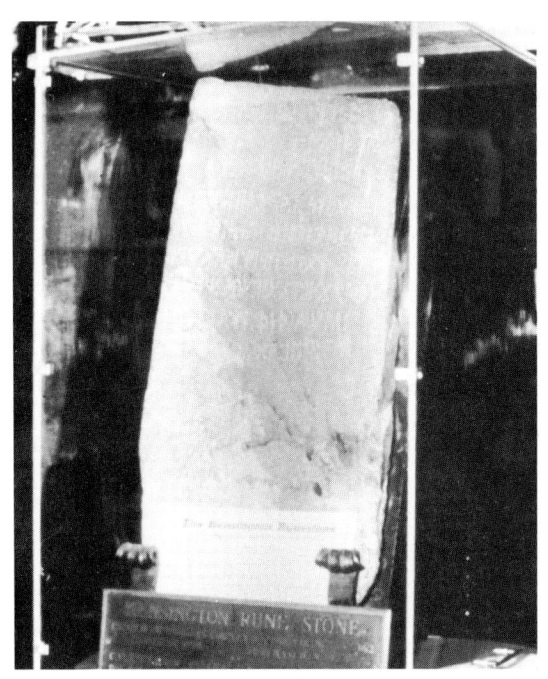

Reproduction of the Kensington Runestone

EARLY GROWTH

Naturally, trading posts sprang up. In 1727 Fort Beauharnois was raised on Lake Pepin's west shore. Fort St. Charles on the Northwest Angle was built in 1732 by the Verendryes.

However, French control ended with their defeat by the British, who took over in 1763.

By 1768 the most important of all the

trading posts had been established at Grand Portage. The Northwest Company used this as their principal headquarters. Furs traded by the Indians were brought by the voyageurs from as far as 1,500 miles away.

Grand Portage has been described as a "metropolis in the wilderness, even boasting French fashions."

In the treaty ending the American Revolution, at Benjamin Franklin's insistence the northern border was placed above the one proposed by the British at the 45th parallel. This gave Minnesota much of its present valuable northern reaches.

As early as 1787, Congress organized the Northwest Territory, including eastern Minnesota. The Louisiana Purchase of 1803 brought the west to U.S. control.

In 1805 Lt. Zebulon Pike and his troops were sent up the Mississippi to explore and subdue the Indians.

Pike assembled a group of Indians at Leech Lake. To demonstrate that America now controlled the area, he raised the American flag with great ceremony and had the British flag shot down.

However, American control was not completely recognized until several years after the War of 1812.

In 1819 Colonel Henry Leavenworth was assigned the task of building a fort at the junction of the Minnesota and Mississippi rivers. He built some log buildings, but his successor, Colonel Josiah Snelling, started a fort on a cliff above the rivers, and this was completed by 1824 and named Fort Snelling in the Colonel's honor the next year.

This remote outpost brought some security to the area, and settlers began to come in.

The coming of the first steamboat in 1823 provided a great boost for the region's growth. The Indians were amazed. When the snorting monster "roared," even strong braves fled.

The Sioux and Chippewa continued their rivalry, and the last battle between the two groups took place as late as 1858.

Meanwhile a number of missionaries to the Indians had set up schools, worked out written alphabets and tried to help the native peoples in many ways.

In 1838 Minneapolis' present site had only one cabin, that of Franklin Steele. Pierre Bottineau claimed land next to Steele's in 1844, and the two men owned most of the land on which the present city is built.

Until this period, Minnesota had been governed under various territories. Finally, in 1849, the Territory of Minnesota was organized, with St. Paul as the capital and Alexander Ramsey as territorial governor. A month went by before the ice went out and a steamboat was able to bring the news of the new territory to St. Paul.

A MIDDLE PERIOD

In the 1850's treaties with the Indians opened much of the state to settlement.

THAT'S CURIOUS:
Pierre "Pig's Eye" Parrant built a cabin on the present site of St. Paul in 1838. Although he was not a very pleasant character, other settlers called the community Pig's Eye. Fortunately, Father Lucian Galtier built a chapel in honor of St. Paul and persuaded the people to change the name to St. Paul.

By 1857 the population had grown enough for statehood to be considered, but Congress waited until a slave state could be paired with Minnesota. Minnesota became the 32nd state on May 11, 1858.

Before that date, the new state had been a part of three empires and nine different territories.

By the time of statehood southeastern Minnesota was fairly well settled. To the west, Litchfield, Hutchinson, and Glencoe were growing communities. New Ulm was protected by Fort Ridgely, and the wilderness settlements of Sauk Centre and Alexandria had their own stockades. There was even an isolated settlement at Duluth.

Prairie life was hard. In areas where there was little timber, the people cut foot-long chunks of sod and used them as building "bricks" to make sod houses. When some of the sod houses were built partly beneath the surface, the builders were pioneering in an energy conservation technique that is popular today.

In 1860 in its first national election, Minnesota voted for Abraham Lincoln.

When Civil War came, troops from distant Minnesota took part in some of the earliest battles in the east. Minnesota regiments took part in many later battles. The First Regiment played a key role in the Battle of Gettysburg.

With more than 20,000 men and women serving on distant battle fronts, in 1862 the home front was wide open to attack by the Indians.

Chief Little Crow and his 1,500 warriors decided that this was the best time to strike back at the settlers and try to regain their lost lands.

They swept across an area fifty miles wide and 200 miles long, killing whole families and taking prisoners.

Fort Ridgely was attacked but held out bravely. Twelve hundred people took refuge at New Ulm, where 500 Indians attacked about 100 defenders. During the night the people assembled a "cannon" from stovepipe. The Indians had a great fear of cannon. When the second attack came, the defenders "fired" the cannons by pounding on anvils, and the Indians fled.

Under the command of H.H. Sibley, a great friend of the Indians and an expert on Indian affairs, the poorly armed Minnesota troops defeated Little Crow's forces at Wood Lake. Nearly 2,000 Indians were taken prisoner and 269 white captives set free. Six hundred settlers had lost their lives.

For their "crimes" against the settlers, 38 Indian prisoners were hanged at one time; this was the largest official execution in the country's history.

Christian Chief Taopi and John Other Day, also a Christian, helped the white settlers, and Day was given $2,500 by the government for his help. All but 25 of the Sioux were removed.

A MODERN STATE

The Lake of the Woods boundary was finally established in 1876.

During the 1880's many internal improvements in flood control and other advances were made, including the Upper Mississippi Reservoir System.

On the Mississippi at Lake Pepin the steamer Seawing capsized in 1890 in a great storm. Ninety-eight people lost their lives. Even more devastating was the forest fire around Hinckley when more than 400 were killed.

Hero of the blaze was railroad engineer Jim Root who backed his train through flames and across a bridge to save 350 passengers and crew. The throttle became so hot his hands fused to it.

The year 1905 was a proud one for the state. The great capitol was dedicated.

Conservationist President Theodore Roosevelt set aside the huge Superior National Forest in 1909.

World War I called 123,325 Minnesota men and women to the country's uniform.

Drought, depression, and dust storms of the 1930's made life hard for Minnesotans, especially the many farmers.

Perhaps in answer to the hard times, the Farmer-Labor Party won most of the major federal and state offices in the election of 1936.

More than 6,000 Minnesotans gave their lives during World War II.

Just after the war the Chippewa tribe began an effort to reclaim some of their rights, and some response was made.

With the opening of the St. Lawrence Seaway in 1959, the inland ports of Minnesota on Lake Superior were opened to the Atlantic by way of the St. Lawrence River.

Fort Snelling had been discontinued as a military base, but in 1961 the historic site became a state park, and the old buildings were saved.

During the 1970's the state benefitted greatly from new methods of handling the iron ore known as taconite. Until the new processes were devised, this ore had been considered useless.

In 1977 Minnesota's own Walter Mondale became the nation's Vice President, and in the election of 1984 he lost

PEOPLES

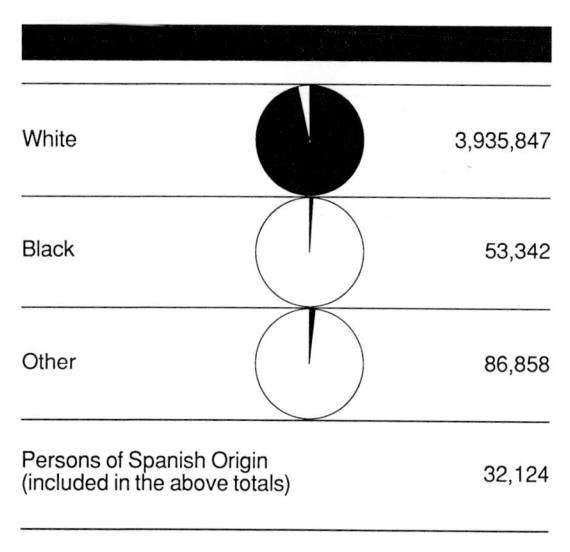

White		3,935,847
Black		53,342
Other		86,858
Persons of Spanish Origin (included in the above totals)		32,124

his bid for the presidency.

Minnesota has become known as the "second Scandinavia." Swedish, Danish, Norwegian, and Finnish settlers arrived in large numbers.

Today there are 27 pages of Johnsons in the Minneapolis phone book, along with 19 pages of Andersons. As someone remarked, "How Swede it is!" However, with many other peoples and races, the Scandinavian population is now only about 12 percent of the total.

PERSONALITIES

One of Minnesota's most prominent modern public figures was Hubert H. Humphrey, whose career covered 32 years of public service, including four years as vice president.

After a notable career in the Senate, Humphrey was nominated as Democratic candidate for president in the 1968 Democratic convention in Chicago. Despite riots in the streets and confusions in the hall, Senator Humphrey received the call on the first ballot.

The election was so close that the lead changed hands several times during the night. It was not known until the day after the election that Richard Nixon had won a narrow victory.

Minnesota's first state governor, Henry Hastings Sibley, was a remarkable early leader. He gained a reputation as the "last of the great fur dealers." Traveling widely as a fur trader, he became one of the top experts in the state's geography and natural history; he treated the Indians fairly; he liked them and they respected him.

At his own expense, Sibley once saved a group of Indians from starving, traveling through heavy snow and reaching them with supplies. He was saddened when circumstances forced him to lead the fight against the Sioux during the Civil War.

In other fields of public service, Mrs. Eugenie Anderson became the first American woman to serve as an ambassador. Senator/Ambassador Frank B. Kellogg won the Nobel Peace Prize for his Kellogg-Briand Peace Pact. William O. Douglas was one of the most controversial of recent Supreme Court justices. Chief Justice Warren Burger also is a Minnesotan.

Charles A. Lindbergh, Jr., came from a prominent Minnesota family. His solo flight across the Atlantic for the first time, made him one of the most prominent and respected figures of his day.

"Empire Builder" James J. Hill received that title because his railroad and real estate holdings helped to develop America's northwest empire.

Other tycoons included John Sargent Pillsbury, whose milling business developed into one of the world's largest food operations, mining tycoon A.M. Chisholm, George Nelson Dayton of Minneapolis department store fame, and lumber baron Frederick Weyerhauser.

Perhaps unique in world history is the famed Mayo family.

Dr. William Worrell Mayo arrived at Le Sueur from England in 1855. After the Mayo family moved to Rochester, the doctor practiced medicine, often with help from his two young sons, William J. and Charles.

After brushing up on his medical knowledge in New York, the senior Mayo became even more popular in Rochester. The Catholic Sisters of St. Francis built a hospital and placed him in charge.

His fame brought many young doctors to study and observe his methods. Dr. Mayo was a genius in organizing medical procedures, in training of doctors and nurses, and in coordinating all of the health facilities and operations.

Today the Mayo clinic has a staff of more than 200 of the most skilled doctors in their fields, along with all of the other staff and facilities that make it one of the world's major health centers.

Dr. Mayo, Sr., received many honors when he toured the world at the age of 87. He died in 1911 at the age of ninety-two. Both the Mayo sons went on to promi-

---

THAT'S CURIOUS:
Young Charles Mayo helped his father by standing on a box and administering ether to patients when he was only nine years old.

Split Rock Lighthouse on Lake Superior illustrates the state's resource of natural beauty and assists transportation

nence as leaders in the clinic.

Sauk Centre, the boyhood home of Sinclair Lewis, provided much of the background for the writings of the Nobel Prize winner.

F. Scott Fitzgerald, Ole Edvart Rolvaag, and Thorstein Veblen were also prominent authors from Minnesota.

A WEALTH OF NATURE

Some of the world's richest mineral treasures have been found in Minnesota.

Iron ores, among the finest anywhere, have been known since Indian times. Manganese of the state is found in one of its greatest deposits. The peat resources are the largest in the country. Pipestone, the Indian treasure, is found only in Minnesota.

Building stone, shale, mica, Thompsonite, and feldspar are among the other minerals found.

The eastern half of Minnesota was almost entirely covered with forests, including the state tree, Norway pine. This unusual tree is not harmed either by insects or disease.

Cypripedium reginae is the state flower. This rare type of orchid is more commonly known as lady's slipper. It can only grow with the help of a small fungus to bring it nourishment from the soil.

Two other rare flowers, Indian pipes and fringed gentian, are favorites of botanists.

One of the most useful plants is wild rice, still so precious to the Indians.

The wonderful woodlands, lakes, rivers, and prairies provide unequalled hunting and fishing opportunities. Minnesota licenses more hunters and fishermen than any other state.

USING THE WEALTH

Minnesota's iron ore was particularly important because it was so near Lake Superior, where it could be cheaply transported. It could easily be brought together with coal from the Midwest for making iron and steel products.

One of the greatest of all iron sources was the Mesabi Range. At first, experts were sure that the ore could not be worked because it was too loose to support mining tunnels.

However, Mesabi developer Leonidas Merrit devised the "open pit" method. He simply removed the debris from the top and scooped out the ore. The Mesabi ores proved to be the richest in history.

As the ores came out, some of the pits became the largest man made holes anywhere, and Minnesota became the national iron mining capital.

The best grade ores have been used up. However, a low-grade ore known as taconite is now mined profitably because of new processing methods devised at University of Minnesota Mines Experiment Station.

In agriculture, the Red River Valley produced so much wheat that Minneapolis became the "Flour City of the World." That title now has to be shared with others, but the city still boasts the largest concentration of major grain milling companies.

As early as 1890, Minnesota had become the nation's leading lumber producing state. This title also moved elsewhere, but timber and pulp are still important. Pulp is manufactured into paper in many state mills. Matchwood, lumber, railroad ties, poles, posts, veneer and Christmas trees all flow from the state's timber operations.

Although wheat and other crops are important, livestock accounts today for more than half of the state's farm income.

In addition to milling, Minnesota has other manufacturing giants, including Minnesota Mining and Manufacturing and Minneapolis-Honeywell, and the world's largest manufacturer of calendars. The Twin Cities also rank high in electronics industries.

THE ECONOMY

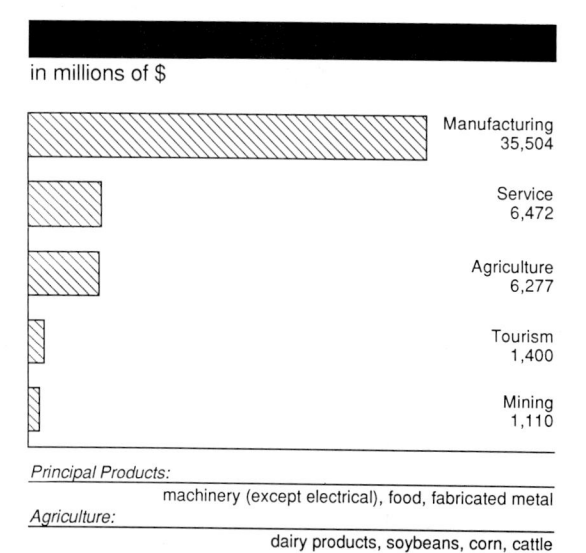

in millions of $

Manufacturing	35,504
Service	6,472
Agriculture	6,277
Tourism	1,400
Mining	1,110

Principal Products: machinery (except electrical), food, fabricated metal
Agriculture: dairy products, soybeans, corn, cattle

GETTING AROUND

Although there are dozens of so-called "twin cities" in the U.S., most people think first of Minneapolis and St. Paul as the Twin Cities.

The Urban Institute of Washington, D.C., has ranked the Twin Cities first among all cities in the country for the overall quality of life. This ranking includes quality of housing, education, shopping, job opportunities, and cultural quality and variety.

There has always been rivalry between the cities on the opposite sides of the Mississippi. There still is, but most of it is friendly.

Many attractions of the area can be

THAT'S CURIOUS:
Cuyler Adams found the last of the great Minnesota iron ranges. He called it the Cuyuna Range. He took the first three letters of his first name — Cuy — and combined them with his dog's name — Una — and gave the range its name.

Minneapolis at night—the Piper Building

claimed jointly by the two cities, such as Fort Snelling State Park, now a national landmark. Metropolitan Stadium, home of the Minnesota Twins baseball team, was placed in neutral territory at Bloomington.

Minneapolis, "The commercial and cultural capital of the Midwest," is a modern city with splendid skyscrapers and great manufacturing and financial headquarters. Because of the cold winters, the city has featured a series of enclosed downtown walkways and bridges, making 14 blocks of the city accessible under roof. Crystal Court Square is an entire block under glass.

Almost from its beginning Minneapolis was a pioneer in the arts. Famed theater expert Sir Tyrone Guthrie began the world-renowned theater that bears his name. The Children's Theater has been called the finest of its kind in the country. The Minnesota Symphony Orchestra has held top-ranking almost from its beginnings in 1903. Throughout the summer various groups give free concerts in the city parks.

One of the most modern of all libraries as well as museums and architecture all add to the city's cultural appeal.

Minnehaha Falls takes its name from the Indians' "laughing waters" and is a principal tourist attraction.

One of the country's major annual festivals is the Winter Carnival at St. Paul, founded in 1886. It features King Boreas and the Queen of the Snows. There are ice-carving contests, and the "500 Snowmobile Race."

Principal attraction for visitors to St. Paul is the massive capitol. Its unsupported marble dome is called the largest of its kind in the world. The building, designed by noted architect Cass Gilbert, has long been considered one of the outstanding state capitols.

Other major St. Paul architecture includes the outstanding Cathedral of St. Paul and the mammoth City Hall, with its Indian Peace Memorial Statue by international sculptor Carl Milles.

The modern Civic Arts and Science Center is home to a wide variety of scientific and cultural institutions.

The Capital Centre redevelopment project encompasses eight city blocks, connected by climate-controlled walkways.

Pipestone National Monument is unique. The red stone found nowhere else is still reserved exclusively to the Indians by federal law.

Another natural attraction is the Canyon of the St. Croix River, sometimes called "The Switzerland of America." One of the principal natural landmarks along the Mississippi is Sugar Loaf Monolith at Winona.

The largest cavern in the midwest is Niagara Cave, near Harmony. A farmer discovered it by accident when a pig fell into it and he heard it squealing.

Despite its relatively small size, Rochester is a city of international importance because of the vast medical and research facilities that grew up there in response to the pioneering Mayo family.

Duluth is a City in a Rock Garden, perched high on the rocky bluffs above Lake Superior. The magnificent harbor at Duluth is protected by a six-mile sandbar. The only natural entrance to the harbor was in Wisconsin. When Duluth decided to cut a channel through the sandbar, Wisconsin appealed. Just before they could be stopped, most of the citizens had worked with a steam shovel and completed the new harbor entrance.

After the ice has broken up, the arrival of the first boat at Duluth is heralded by everyone.

One of the most scenic areas in the Midwest is found on the lake circle route along the Lake Superior shore to the Canadian border.

Grand Portage National Monument is a re-creation of the busy days when the area was a center of civilization in a wilderness.

The largest city in the western half of Minnesota is Moorhead. It is the metropolis of the wide-open spaces of the Red River Valley.

A contrast is found in the forest wilderness to the north, including vast Superior-Quetico primitive region, jointly maintained by the U.S. and Canada. Here, in addition to the hydroplane, canoe, skiing, snowshoeing, and hiking are the only means of travel. Ely is the jumping-off place for this area.

Much of the rest of north and central Minnesota provides wonderful opportunities for outdoor recreation in woodlands and on streams and the multitudes of lakes.

Visitors find much to attract them in the many forestry and iron mining communities, especially the open pit canyons of the Mesabi Range.

Brainard calls itself the home of Paul Bunyan, with its annual Paul Bunyan Carnival and the largest animated statue of the legendary hero. Another statue of Bunyan with his blue ox Babe stands at Bemidji.

For many visitors the most moving natural attraction in the state is Itasca State Park, where they make their way across the narrow and shallow beginning of the mighty Mississippi crossing only on stepping-stones.

COMPAC-FACS

MINNESOTA
Gopher State - North Star State
HISTORY
Statehood: May 11, 1858
Admitted as: 32nd state
Capital: St. Paul, settled 1840
OFFICIAL SYMBOLS
Motto: L'Etoile du Nord ("The Star of the North")
Slogan: Land of 10,000 Lakes
Bird: Common loon (gavia immer)
Fish: Walleye (stizostidion vitrium)
Flower: Pink and white lady's slipper (cypripedium reginae)
Tree: Red pine (Norway), (pinus resinosa)

The grand capitol

Gem: Lake Superior agate
Song: "Hail! Minnesota"
GEO-FACS
Area: 79,548 sq. mi.
Rank in Area: 12th
Length (n/s): 405 mi.
Width (e/w): 384 mi.
Geographic Center: 10 mi. sw of Brainerd
Highest Point: 1,979 ft. (Mt. Arvon)
Lowest Point: 702 ft. (Lake Superior)
Mean Elevation: 900 ft.
Temperature, Extreme Range: 173 degrees
Number of Counties: 87
POPULATION
Total: 4,144,000 (1983)
Rank: 21st
Density: 52 persons per sq. mi.
Principal Cities: Minneapolis, 370,951; St. Paul, 270,230; Duluth, 92,811; Bloomington, 81,831; Rochester, 57,890; Edina, 46,073
EDUCATION
Schools: 2,137 elementary and secondary
Higher: 70
VITAL STATISTICS
Births (1980/83): 223,000
Deaths (1980/83): 109,000
Hospitals: 182
Drinking Age: 19
INTERESTING PEOPLE
Hubert H. Humphrey, Sinclair Lewis, Henry Hastings Sibley, Eugenie Anderson, Frank B. Kellogg, William O. Douglas, Warren Burger, Charles A. Lindbergh, F. Scott Fitzgerald, E.G. Marshall, William Worrell Mayo, Sr., Charles Mayo, William J. Mayo, Charles Schulz, Harold Stassen, Thorstein Veblen
WHEN DID IT HAPPEN?
1679: Duluth claims area for France
1689: St. Antoine builds first trading fort
1763: British rule begins
1796: Portion of Minnesota included in Northwest Territory
1805: Pike explores
1820: Fort Snelling commenced
1823: Fort Snelling greets first steamboat
1849: Minnesota Territory created
1858: Minnesota becomes a state
1862: Sioux war
1884: Iron ore shipments begin
1932: Discovery of "Minnesota Man"
1978: Death of Hubert Humphrey
1984: Walter F. Mondale defeated for presidency

MISSOURI

FASCINATING MISSOURI

The incidents and episodes and facts that bring the story of Missouri to life are as varied as giving birth to the iron curtain as well as giving birth to an "extra" U.S. president.

Geographically, Missouri is the state with the most neighbors, the biggest boot heel, the most caves and the largest springs.

Its history tells the story of the 14-year-old boy who founded its greatest city, and prehistory indicates that boy chose the site of a great ancient metropolis which traded with distant peoples.

Missouri history also records the "war" over honey, the only General of the Armies of the U.S., the "giant" Indians, the troublesome pirates, and the worst earthquake ever to strike this country.

Certainly not the least interesting is the confusion of the two Winston Churchills.

THE FACE OF MISSOURI

Only one other state has as many neighboring states as Missouri, which links borders with eight states: Iowa, Kansas, Nebraska, Arkansas, Oklahoma, Illinois, Kentucky, and Tennessee.

Two of the country's greatest rivers influence much of the state, particularly where the mighty Mississippi and the turbulent Missouri join. For some distance the two rivers appear to flow almost separately, with the muddy waters of the Missouri clinging to the west side, until finally the waters merge completely. Both these rivers are apt to change their channels, sometimes overnight. This has created much confusion when boundaries are involved and chunks of one state suddenly end up across the river in another state.

Other major rivers are the Black, White, St. Francis and Osage. The strangely shaped portion of Missouri known as The Heel is formed between the St. Francis and Mississippi rivers.

Missouri is noted for its many enormous springs, about 500 in all. The world's largest single-outlet spring is Big Springs near Van Buren. Each day, 846,000,000 gallons pour out of its mouth.

For the number of large caves, Missouri probably holds the record. The public may enter twenty-six of these. Several natural bridges provide arches of interest to both traveler and geologist.

Missouri's many major lakes are nearly all man-made. Lake of the Ozarks has, perhaps, the most widespread reputation of any. Lake Taneycomo and Bull Shoals Lake are also very popular.

Prehistoric Missouri must have been vastly different.

At one time the Gulf of Mexico probably extended to where the Mississippi and Ohio rivers meet. Much of the land south of that is actually part of the delta of the Mississippi, formed by the trillions of tons of mud and debris washed down by the great river system. This area is called the Mississippi Embayment.

The many high and rugged hills and bluffs tower above the lowlands in several areas and give a mountainous appearance to highlands such as the Missouri Ozarks.

A number of important fossils have been found in the state, including those of mastodons and elephants, discovered near Kimmswick.

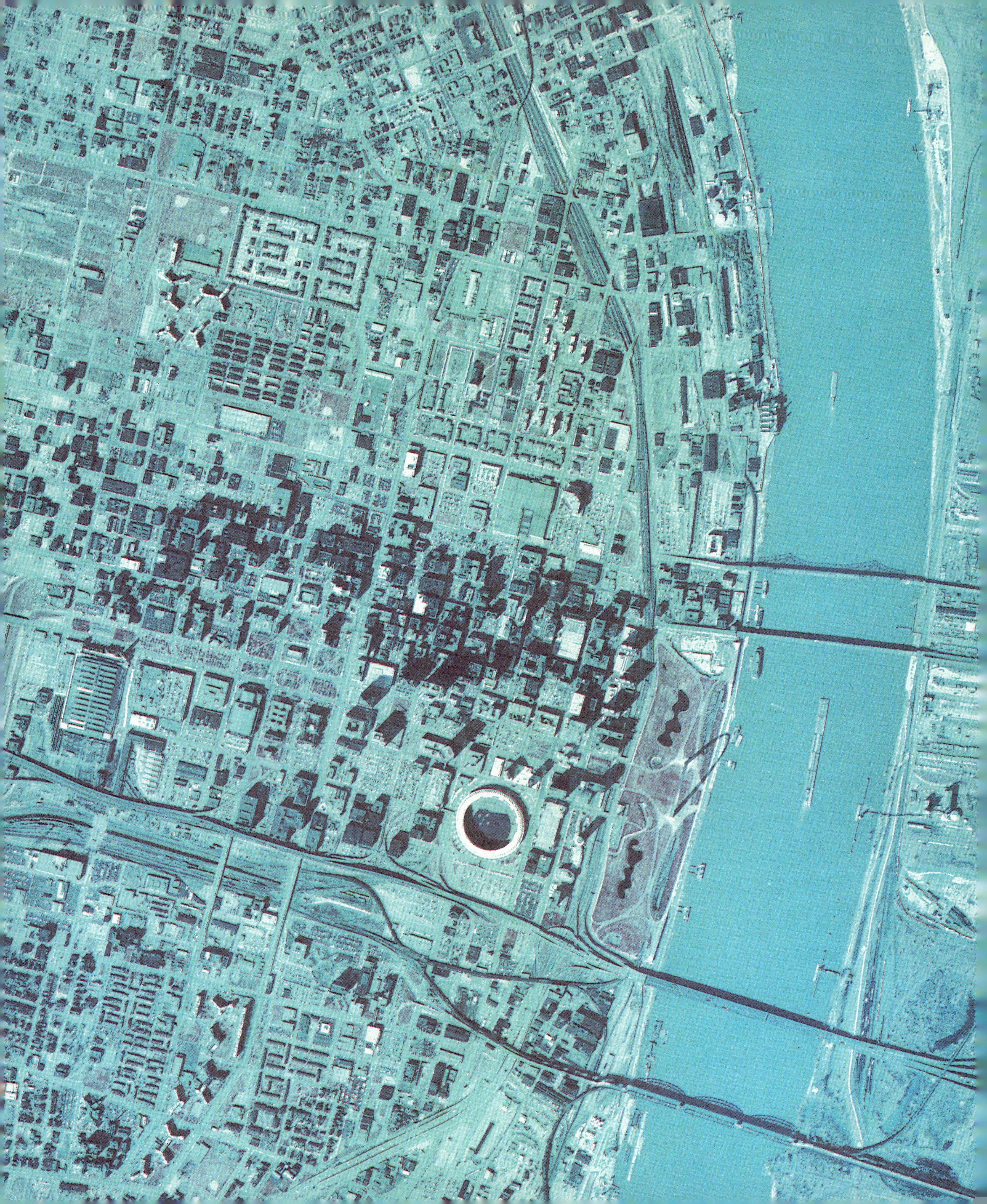

THAT'S CURIOUS:
The prehistoric metropolitan center of Old Village flourished on the exact site of present St. Louis. Apparently the locale held the same attraction for city planners then as now. Similarly, at about the same time as Old Village another great community was thriving on the site of present Kansas City.

EARLY DWELLERS

Depending on which authority is accepted, people have lived in the Missouri area from 10,000 to 30,000 years.

The first discovery of its kind in America was made at the Bourbeuse River area by Albrecht Kock. In 1838 he found human remains among the bones of mastodons, showing that humans had been there at the same time as the prehistoric animals. This discovery was made only two years later than the same kind of finding in Europe.

The people who lived in Graham Cave, Montgomery County, about 10,000 years ago are known as Early Man. Those following are called Archaic Man, Woodland Man and Mississippi Man.

Visitors and traders came to prehistoric Old Village from the far reaches of the Mississippi Valley and beyond. Jewelry, tooled copper in the form of eagles and human heads, hair ornaments of bones, pottery, and woodwork were created there.

Trade was probably carried on with places as far away as Mexico. The ancient peoples left many remnants of their civilization in the mounds of earth they piled up.

The main Indian groups in the early historical period were the Osage of the south and west, the Missouri of the northwest and a few Ioway to the north and east.

(Opposite) St. Louis by NAHP/EROS

The Osage were remarkable for their physical appearance; the average height of a male was probably over six feet. Many were over seven feet in height. Early scientists who were familiar with them called their physical condition "incredible." They were frequently known to walk 60 miles a day.

Before the women and children began the tasks of the day, they painted the part in their hair a red color. This was the symbol of the sun's path as it passed the day, a hope of long life.

The Osage carried on warfare almost continuously, but they also cared for the sick and aged.

They were familiar with simple aspects of medicine and science.

Perhaps most remarkable of all, the Osage were not greatly influenced by European ways. Even the alcoholic drinks that so damaged other tribes seemed to have little effect on Osage people.

About early European exploration, one authority writes, "...There seems little reason to doubt that (Hernando) De Soto and his band...reached their 'farthest north' among the granitic knobs of the St. Francois Mountains in what is now Iron County."

Other historians believe that Francisco de Coronado reached present Missouri from the west at about the same time. Others feel that the two exploring parties may even have met some time in August, 1541.

There is no doubt however, that De

The founders would be astonished to see St. Louis today. The great Gateway Arch symbolizes Missouri's role as "Gateway to the West"

Soto's party brought diseases against which the Indians had no immunity, leaving a terrible legacy of health problems for many generations.

There is also no doubt about the record of the visit of explorers Father Jacques Marquette and Louis Jolliet. They discovered the mouth of the Missouri and other parts of the state in 1673.

In 1682 French explorer Robert Cavelier, Sieur de La Salle, skirted the Missouri shores on his way to the Mississippi's mouth; traders and other travelers must have visited the area both before and after that time.

French Jesuit missionaries founded the first European settlement in present Missouri, St. Francis Xavier Mission, in 1700, but it was abandoned three years later.

Several attempts to find mineral riches in the region failed, and there were no permanent European settlements in Missouri until 1735, when Ste. Genevieve was begun.

St. Louis was established in 1764.

Just before the French were defeated by the British in 1763, they had ceded their Louisiana territory to the Spanish, who took over the Missouri area.

EARLY GROWTH

The fur trade increased greatly, and St. Louis became the center of both trade and culture for the vast interior region.

During the American Revolution, the Spanish gave aid to the Americans. When St. Louis was attacked by 1,000 Indians and some white traders sympathetic to the British, 50 soldiers and 250 townspeople held off the attack. The British failed to control the important Mississippi supply route.

However, river pirates plagued the settlements until their defeat in 1788.

Spain had liberal policies about settlement in its territories, and the number of Americans living on the west side of the Mississippi grew rapidly.

THAT'S CURIOUS:
The founder of St. Louis was a boy not quite fourteen years old. He was Auguste Chouteau, chosen by and perhaps the son of Pierre Laclede Liguest, head of the fur monopoly of the area. Chouteau led a large expedition up the Mississippi and Ohio, and personally chose the site of the present great city.

Then, in 1800, Spain surrendered the entire Louisiana Territory to Napoleon, who closed the Mississippi to Americans. When Americans went to Paris to protest, they were given the surprising offer to buy the entire territory from France; by 1803 all Louisiana Territory was owned by the U.S.

In a sprightly ceremony at St. Louis on March 9, 1804, America took over the upper portion of Louisiana Territory and placed it under Indiana Territory. A year later Missouri was placed under Louisiana Territory.

One of the great events of history was the formation of the Lewis and Clark expedition at St. Louis and the beginning of their great journey in 1804 up the treacherous Missouri River, as well as their triumphal return in 1805.

Fort Osage at present Kansas City was set up in 1808 as the first American outpost in the present state. It was established to assist the Osage against the other Indian tribes.

Many Indian groups displaced in the East had come to Missouri, including Cherokee, Piankashaw, Kickapoo, Delaware, Wea, and Michigamea. They feared the coming of white settlers would displace them again, and there were Indian attacks, especially in the War of 1812.

By 1816 peace had come, and by 1837 the last of the Indians had been pushed from Missouri, even including the proud Osage, who were moved into Kansas.

One of the most horrendous natural events in the country's history was the great earthquake of 1811, centered at New Madrid. New lakes were formed, rivers changed course, islands disappeared, and heavy quakes continued for

Thomas Hart Benton depicted friendly Indians for his mural at the Truman library

almost two years.

Missouri Territory was created in 1812. Six years later Missouri had sufficient population to become a state. Those opposed to slavery did not want a new slave state, so admission was delayed. Finally Congress admitted slave state Missouri along with free state Maine. In an agreement known as the Missouri Compromise, slavery would be outlawed north of 36 degrees and 30 minutes north latitude.

Missouri was admitted to statehood by President James Monroe on August 10, 1821.

During the years that followed, Missouri became the gateway to all of the west. St. Louis and later Kansas City and St. Joseph were the assembly points for the thousands of traders and settlers who

The Pony Express symbolizes St. Joseph's role in westward expansion, painting by Charles Hargems

went across the Santa Fe, the Oregon and other trails to the Southwest, the West and the Northwest.

As early as 1844, a wagon train of 800 people had moved out of St. Joseph to California.

When gold was found in California, the hordes of people rushing through Missouri could hardly be believed. The money they all spent helped Missouri grow and prosper.

One of the saddest episodes in Missouri's history is the treatment of the Mormons, who had been driven to Missouri from the east. They built a splendid town called Far West and became very successful.

Because of their success and their different religious beliefs, they became hated by those around them. An order was even given for the army to execute the leaders, but the order was fortunately ignored.

When the last groups of the Mormons were driven out, their foes destroyed Far West, leaving only a bare field.

Even greater hatred was aroused over the crime of slavery.

One of the most famous of all court cases began in St. Louis in 1847 when Dred Scott went to court to gain his freedom from slavery. The U.S. Supreme Court finally ruled that a slave had no right to sue in court. However, Dred Scott was freed by his "master."

Nearby Kansas and Nebraska were to choose whether they would be slave or free. Missouri was greatly divided over the issue. In the rivalry for Kansas, pro- and anti-slave groups attacked each other.

However, when the Civil War came, most Missourians were opposed to secession by the South.

During the war both sides were desperate to take Missouri and gain control of the Mississippi. After many battles, Union forces took control of the state in 1862.

However, the guerilla warfare that followed brought constant turmoil. The "total war" fought by the guerillas "...made a real contribution to the Confederate war effort in the West...The fierceness and fury of this war appalled all Missourians, and touched most of them personally."

In 1864 Confederate forces again invaded, almost won, but were driven back after the bloody battle of Westport, known as "the Gettysburg of the West." This battle is said to have "saved the west for the Union."

More than 10 percent of all the battles of the Civil War, 1,100 in all, were fought in Missouri.

In 1865 Missouri became the first slave state to free its slaves. Because it had remained loyal to the Union, the state did not suffer the horrors of "Reconstruction."

Many of the guerillas turned bandit after the war. Most famous of these were the outlaws led by Jesse James, who was murdered at St. Joseph for the $10,000 reward. Belle Starr was a feared Missouri woman outlaw who was shot in Texas.

UP-TO-DATE

The first national convention west of the Mississippi came to St. Louis in 1876, where the Democrats nominated Samuel J. Tilden.

The St. Louis Symphony was founded in 1880, and in the more than 100 years since, it has become one of the nation's finest.

One of the longest lasting of all state border fights began in 1839 and was not settled until 1896 by the U.S. Supreme Court. Iowa and Missouri had almost gone to war over that dispute.

When a fire in Kansas City in 1900 destroyed the convention hall, it appeared the Democratic convention could not be held there. However, the people went to work and within three months the building was ready, and William Jennings Bryan was nominated.

St. Louis held world attention in 1904 with its grand Louisiana Purchase Exposition, a world's fair to honor the purchase of that territory. It is thought the ice-cream cone originated at the fair.

In World War I, American forces overseas were led by General John J. Pershing of Missouri.

In World War II Missouri produced other world leaders, including Generals James H. Doolittle and Omar M. Bradley.

However, another Missouri man became the most prominent of all when Harry S. Truman, native of Lamar, became president on the death of Franklin D. Roosevelt in 1945.

In 1946 the great British war leader Winston Churchill came to Westminster College at Fulton, Missouri. There he gave the famous speech in which he said, "...An Iron Curtain has descended across the Continent (of Europe)."

In 1966 the nation celebrated when the Gateway Arch was dedicated at St. Louis as part of Jefferson National Expansion Memorial. This extraordinary monument has become the symbol of the opening and development of the West.

The year 1985 sparked other memories. Ste. Genevieve celebrated the 250th anniversary of its founding and Hannibal spent much of the year remembering its native son Samuel Clemens (Mark Twain) on the 150th anniversary of his birth.

PERSONALITIES

When Harry S. Truman became president, he had not even been told

---

THAT'S CURIOUS:
The Iowa-Missouri border dispute came to be called the Honey War. The wild bee honey trees found in the disputed area were greatly prized because there was such a shortage of sweetenings.

THAT'S CURIOUS:
In honor of Churchill's "Iron Curtain" speech a London church of the 12th century, redesigned by Christopher Wren in the 1600's, was taken apart and rebuilt at Fulton as the Westminster College chapel.

about the top secret work which had produced the atomic bomb. Suddenly he was faced with one of the most important decisions of historic times. Should the bomb be used in warfare?

His decision to use the bomb was hailed then as it brought World War II to a sudden end, saving millions of lives. However, the decision has become ever more bitterly debated as the years have passed.

When he became president, Truman was very little known to the American people, although he had a distinguished career of service, beginning with World War I and continuing through outstanding work in the U.S. Senate. As vice president he remained in the tremendous shadow of mighty F.D. Roosevelt.

As President his popularity grew, however, and he won the election of 1948. The election was close, and Truman gloated over a Chicago newspaper headline which said he had lost the election.

Truman declined to run in 1952 and retired to his Independence home. The president happily spent his remaining days working on his memoirs and preparing for the Truman library.

The worldwide reputation and respect for President Truman have grown dramatically in the years since he left office, and now some historians rank him among the nation's top chief executives.

Only one American has ever been given the rank of General of the Armies; that was General John Joseph Pershing, born near Laclede in 1860. The West Point graduate had served in the Apache wars, in the Spanish-American War and fought Mexican raiders across the U.S. border.

As commander-in-chief of the American World War I expeditionary forces, he led the American troops in the victory. The rank General of the Armies was created for George Washington, but apparently never used.

Prominent Missouri legislators include Thomas Hart Benton and James Beauchamp (Champ) Clark. Benton had one of the most successful of all senatorial careers; Clark was a leading congressman.

PEOPLES

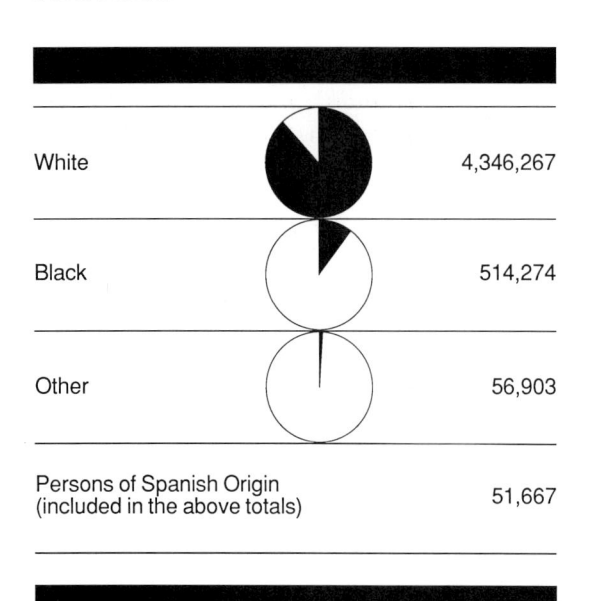

White	4,346,267
Black	514,274
Other	56,903
Persons of Spanish Origin (included in the above totals)	51,667

Samuel Langhorne Clemens is known today as one of America's foremost writers. He gained early fame reporting the wild mining booms of Virginia City and California.

As a pilot on the Mississippi, Sam Clemens would drop a line down to learn the depth of the river. When a certain depth was reached, they would call out "mark twain!" as was the custom. From that call Clemens took the pen name—Mark Twain—which became famous around the world.

Joseph Pulitzer, a native of Hungary, became a prominent publisher of newspapers in St. Louis and New York. His fame is perpetuated through his well-known Pulitzer Prizes in journalism and other literary forms.

The unlikely sounding town of Pumpkin Center was the birthplace of Dale Carnegie, who gained fame for his works on getting ahead in life.

Novelists Harold Bell Wright, Winston Churchill and Fanny Hurst, and poet Eugene Field all gained renown through their writings.

Among the best-known modern artists is Thomas Hart Benton, namesake of his grand-uncle the Senator; he is particularly famed for his many outstanding murals. Artist of an entirely different type was cartoonist Walt Disney who went on to create the great Disney entertainment empire. The characters he animated and the amusement centers he pioneered have made his name one of the best known of modern times.

A very popular composer-entertainer, W.C. Handy, provided a new kind of music with his "St. Louis Blues." By contrast, classical composer Virgil Thompson, native of Kansas City, is one of the most respected in his field.

The brewery founded by Eberhard Anheuser and Adolphus Busch had become the largest in the world as early as 1900. The Busch name is perpetuated in Busch Stadium, home of the St. Louis Cardinals, as well as the various popular Busch gardens.

One of the nation's leading merchants was J.C. Penney, born on a farm outside Breckenridge.

The name of Joyce C. Hall has been carried worldwide on hundreds of millions of greeting cards. At an early time Hall recognized how important the greeting card business might become, and formed the most successful company in the field.

Mr. Hall's enthusiam for Kansas City brought about his building of the outstanding Crown Center complex there. He also pioneered in presenting quality television programs to advertise his products.

Missouri also has close associations with one of America's almost legendary heroes, pathfinder Daniel Boone. At age 65 he came to Missouri to start life over, after losing most of his property in Kentucky.

Boone was given honors and property by the Spanish who ruled the region at the time. Congress confirmed his land

THAT'S CURIOUS:
In addition to Truman, Missouri may be said to have had another "President." Zachary Taylor postponed his inauguration a day for religious reasons. During that day David Rice of Missouri, President pro tempore of the Senate, could be considered the U.S. president.

THAT'S CURIOUS:
When asked if he had ever become lost, Daniel Boone, the wilderness scout, answered, "I was never lost, but I was bewildered once for three days."

---

grants, but his Kentucky creditors swept in and wiped him out again. He returned to trapping for furs to repay his debts.

A notable American scientist, George Washington Carver, native of Diamond, went on to become one of the most renowned black Americans. It is not generally known that his ability as an artist was remarkable.

A WEALTH OF NATURE

The great Missouri lead preserves have been important from early times in the state.

Perhaps even more important are the billions of gallons of petroleum reserves that may be locked in the oil-bearing sands of western Missouri. These still await the practical methods of extraction that will someday undoubtedly be used.

Large coal reserves, lime, sand and gravel, barite, fire clays and iron ore are also available.

About a quarter of the state is still covered with forests, almost twice as much as the neighboring states. The trees cover an amazing variety. One of the rarest is the smoke tree.

Even more numerous are the plants and flowers—more than 2,000 varieties are found in the state, including the purple fringed orchid.

The herds of elk and countless buffalo are gone, but smaller game is still plentiful.

USING THE WEALTH

Manufacturers in Missouri employ nearly half a million workers. McDonnell Aircraft at St. Louis has become the state's largest employer.

Anheuser-Busch still ranks as the world's largest brewery, and Monsanto Chemical Company is another leader in its field.

Trans World and Ozark Airlines are headquartered in the state where so much earlier the Pony Express also originated.

Surprisingly, perhaps, Missouri ranks third among the states in the production and assembly of automobiles. Kansas City is second only to Detroit in automobile assembly.

In agriculture Missouri has more farms than any other state. In 1983 the number exceeded 117,000. Surrounded by the other great agricultural states, Kansas City likes to call itself "Heart of the world's greatest larder."

Cattle and grain bring in the greatest farm revenue.

Crops range from soybeans and tree nuts to tobacco, with the chant of the tobacco auctioneer a familiar sound.

In livestock the state ranks second in number of cattle farms and hog farms.

In a different field St. Louis is still the world's largest raw fur market.

In mineral production Missouri is distinguished by world leadership of lead. In this field it has held top U.S. rank for more than 70 years. Lead production is important for another reason. Zinc, copper and silver are recovered as important co-products of southwestern Missouri's lead mines. The state ranks second in zinc production and sixth in silver.

Coal mining in the state from strip mines produced revenues of more than $148 million in 1982. Sand and gravel are important and Ste. Genevieve boasts the largest independent lime operation in the U.S.

Lumber and wood products bring more than half a billion dollars to the state each year. Among such products, the state leads the nation in charcoal and wood barrel production.

In transportation the state has always held a key position since it became the jumping-off place for the west.

As a modern transport center, St. Louis' combination of rail, highway, waterways and air travel make it second only to Chicago in that field, nor is Kansas City very far behind.

The state experienced one colorful form of transportation after another. Stagecoaches bumped over crude roads; thousands of covered wagons set out for distant destinations; the pony express dashed off, and particularly exciting were the early steamboats.

The huge paddle wheel steamers provided some of the most elegant transportation imaginable, and some remain even today. The exciting steamboat races were celebrated in song and story. Today, though less exciting, the sturdy tugs and barges carry untold thousands of tons of the widest variety of freight on the Mississippi and Missouri.

GETTING AROUND

Led by St. Louis and Kansas City, Missouri offers outstanding tourist attractions.

One of the most dramatic entrances anywhere welcomes those visitors. The Gateway Arch on St. Louis' waterfront

THE ECONOMY

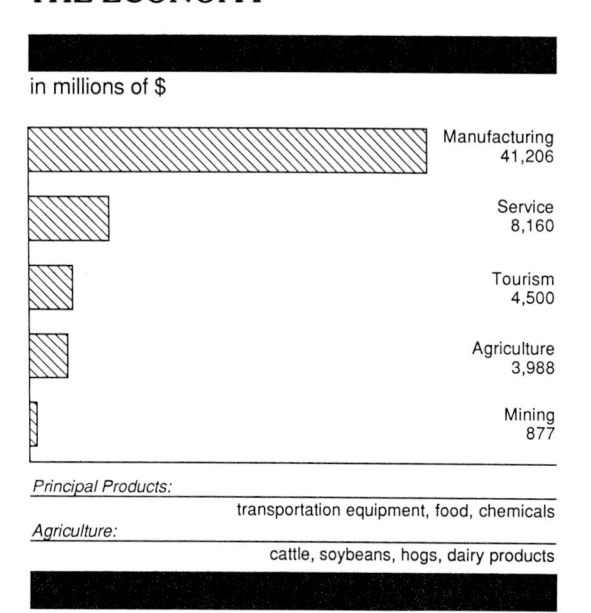

in millions of $

Manufacturing	41,206
Service	8,160
Tourism	4,500
Agriculture	3,988
Mining	877

Principal Products: transportation equipment, food, chemicals
Agriculture: cattle, soybeans, hogs, dairy products

soars in a 630 foot arc, with a thrilling "train ride" to the very top. At its base is the underground Museum of Westward Expansion reminding all of the city's heritage as gateway to the west.

Nearby Laclede's Landing is a revitalized nine-block area of dining and shopping. The Old Cathedral and Old Courthouse are also close at hand.

The great excursion steamboats still collect their passengers near the arch. The St. Louis Centre, the Union Market and St. Louis Station are all evidence of the remarkable resurgence of the downtown.

The art museum, Historical Society Museum, zoo, Science Center, Botanical Gardens, the country's second largest planetarium and the beauty of Forest Park all add to the city's attraction.

The Cardinals at Busch Stadium and other sports attractions and the National

93

Nichols Fountain, Country Club Plaza.

Bowling Hall of Fame and Museum emphasize the city's sporting appeal.

Topping them all is the fabled Veiled Prophet Fair, one of the country's largest Fourth of July festivals.

In eastern and central Missouri are other attractions.

St. Charles lures travelers to its First State Capital historic district with its pioneer capitol. The present capital, Jefferson City, and Columbia offer city amenities in mid-Missouri. Columbia, largest city of the center, is a favorite stop between St. Louis and Kansas City.

That city is one of the most cosmopolitan centers in the nation.

It pioneered in one of America's favorite habits. The dazzling Country Club Plaza, founded by J.C. Nichols, was the very first major shopping center. It still is one of the most elegant anywhere. Crown Center is another imposing hotel-shopping-office complex. One of the three or four greatest collections of Oriental art may be found at the William Rockhill Nelson Gallery of Art.

City Center Square and H. Roe Bartle Exposition Hall hold many attractions. The twin stadia of Harry S. Truman Sports Complex are home to the Kansas City Chiefs and other sports activities.

Notable annual events include the American Royal Livestock and Horse Show.

Just to the east, Independence revels in the memory of Harry Truman, with the Truman Library and family home attracting thousands.

Although the Mormons were driven out by persecution, one branch has returned to Missouri. The headquarters of the Reorganized Church of Jesus Christ of Latter Day Saints is at Independence, with its great auditorium.

To the north, in St. Joseph, the old stables where the Pony Express began provide a highlight.

Springfield and Joplin are twin gateways to all the delights of the Ozarks. The many picturesque lakes, the beauty of the mountains, especially in fall and spring, and such attractions as Silver Dollar City lure thousands of tourists.

Another tourist lure is found in the many caves. Missouri has more of them than any other state. Fantastic Caverns at Springfield is said to be the only cave in America large enough to drive through.

As winter arrives, so do the hundreds of bald eagles who make their homes along the Mississippi River bluffs and elsewhere — a constant reminder to all of the American heritage.

The massive capitol closely resembles the U.S. capitol at Washington

COMPAC-FACS
MISSOURI
Show Me State

HISTORY
Statehood: August 10, 1821
Admitted as: 24th state
Capital: Jefferson City, begun in 1823
OFFICIAL SYMBOLS
Motto: Salus Populi Suprema Lex Esto ("The Welfare of the People Shall be the Supreme Law")
Bird: Eastern bluebird
Flower: Hawthorn blossom
Tree: Flowering dogwood
Song: "Missouri Waltz"
Rock: Mozarkite
Mineral: Galena (lead)
GEO-FACS
Area: 69,697 sq. mi.
Rank in Area: 19th
Length (n/s): 300 mi.
Width (e/w): 280 mi.
Geographic Center: In Miller, 20 mi. sw of Jefferson City
Highest Point: 1,772 ft. (Tom Sauk Mountain)
Lowest Point: 230 ft. (St. Francis River)
Mean Elevation: 800 ft.
Temperature, Extreme Range: 158 degrees
Number of Counties: 114 (plus 1 independent city)
POPULATION
Total: 4,970,000 (1983)
Rank: 15
Density: 72 persons per sq. mi.
Principal Cities: St. Louis, 453,085; Kansas City, 448,159; Springfield, 133,116; Independence, 111,806; Columbia, 62,061; Florissant, 55,372
EDUCATION
Schools: 2,594 elementary and secondary
Higher: 66
VITAL STATISTICS
Births (1980/83): 251,000
Deaths (1980/83): 159,000
Hospitals: 169
Drinking Age: 19

Missouri's many lakes add greatly to the attractions of the state and bring in substantial tourist income

INTERESTING PEOPLE
Harry S. Truman, Thomas Hart Benton (statesman), Thomas Hart Benton (artist), George Washington Carver, Gen. John J. Pershing; Dale Carnegie, Samuel Clemens (Mark Twain), Joseph Pulitzer, Gen. Omar Bradley, Daniel Boone, Adolphus Busch, Walt Disney, Eugene Field, Joyce Hall, W.C. Handy, William Rockhill Nelson, J.C. Penney, Harold Bell Wright

WHEN DID IT HAPPEN?
1541: De Soto and Coronado may have explored
1673: Missouri River discovered by Marquette and Jolliet
1735: First settlement, Sainte Genevieve
1764: St. Louis founded
1770: Formal control by Spanish
1800: France regains control
1803: Louisiana Territory bought by U.S.
1804: Lewis and Clark begin journey
1811: Indian wars
1821: Missouri becomes a state
1843: Great emigration begins
1849: California gold rush
1856: Kansas question brings guerrilla war
1861: Battle of Boonville
1864: Battle of Westport
1880: St. Louis forms now famed symphony
1904: Louisiana Purchase Exposition
1917: World War I begins, 140,257 from Missouri serve
1921: State Centennial celebrated
1941: World War II begins, 450,000 from Missouri serve
1945: Truman becomes President
1966: Gateway Arch dedicated
1976: Kansas City Republican Convention nominates Gerald Ford
1985: 250th anniversary of founding of Sainte Genevieve

OHIO

FASCINATING OHIO

Cleveland, Connecticut? Somehow that doesn't sound quite right. Ohio entered the union in 1953? The Hetuck State? Something wrong there! Those are just a few of the unusual puzzles and interesting facts that emphasize the fascination of the Ohio story.

Consider the fighting bouquet and the fighting cornstalk, the real story of Liza on the ice, the first hot dog, and the "mad" general, the burial of the historic plates.

Marvel at the exploring dog, the three-ended bridge, the man on the moon, the great serpent with a huge egg in its mouth, the accidental soap, and the mechanical money drawer.

Read all about it! And, more seriously, learn about the land, the people and the history that have been brought together in this great state.

THE FACE OF OHIO

After the explorers and early settlers struggled over the eastern mountains, they welcomed the level lands of Ohio as if they formed a gateway leading to the western world. Ever since, Ohio has been known, among other titles, as the Gateway State.

Water transportation provided the easiest early entrance to that gate. The grand Ohio River twists for 450 miles along the entire southern border of the state, while Lake Erie accounts for eastern two thirds of the northern border.

The balance of that eastern border was so important that Ohio and Michigan had a "Border War" to determine

Hocking Hills State Park illustrates Ohio's geographic variety; (Overleaf) Cincinnati by NHAP/EROS

which state owned the area that now includes Toledo. Of course, Ohio won.

Within the state, Ohio has only about 500 lakes, mostly man made. However, the state boasts 44,000 miles of rivers and streams.

Some of the state's rivers which flow into Lake Erie are among the most important in the Great Lakes system, including the Maumee, Portage, Sandusky, Vermillion, Cuyahoga, and Grand.

Flowing to the Ohio River are the Great and Little Miami rivers, the Scioto, Raccoon, Hocking and Muskingum.

Geographers who look closely at the sources of rivers note that water which falls north of a certain line in Ohio flows north to Lake Erie, while the rest flows to the south into the Ohio River. This

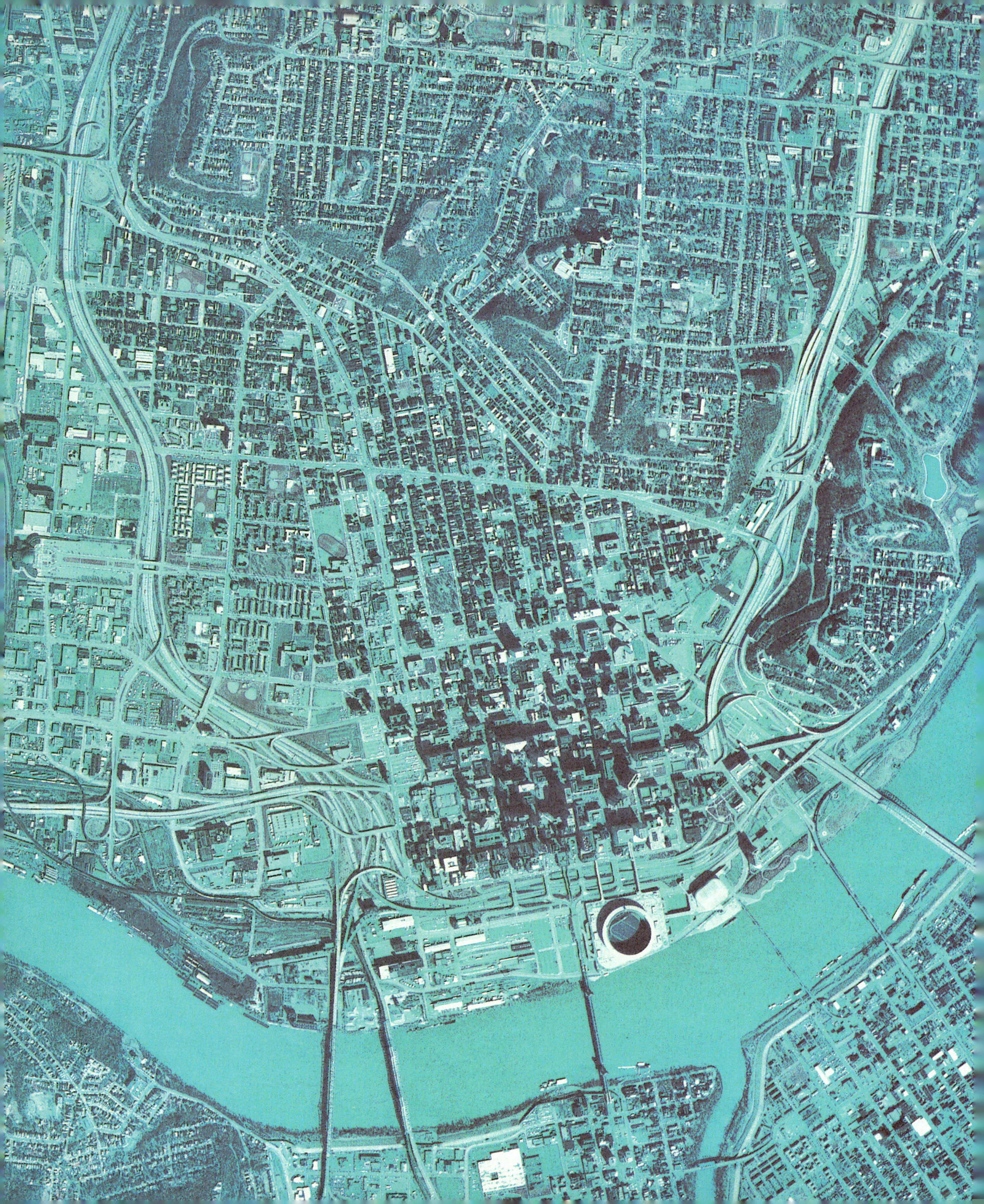

separation of the waters is known as a "divide."

There is another kind of "divide" in Ohio. The forest lands of the east merge into the grassy prairie of the west. This was especially important to the early farmers because the grasslands could be farmed without the difficult labor of clearing away the trees.

Providing variety in the Sandusky area is a small group of islands, including the Bass Islands and Kelleys Island.

In the glacial periods, four great masses of ice moved down from the north. They gouged out new lakes, filled in valleys, brought rich soil and retreated four times, the last about 10,000 years ago. The deep grooves in rocks at Kelleys Island State Park illustrate the force with which the glaciers changed the land.

There is a substantial area of Ohio to the south which was not reached by the glaciers. This looks quite different from the glaciated region.

During much earlier prehistoric periods, shallow seas flowed into a large part of the area and then dried up as the land rose again. Each time the waters left layers of valuable minerals.

Today, five states border on Ohio. The straight man made boundary on the northeast separates Ohio and Pennsylvania. To the east and southeast, the neighbor is West Virginia. The rest of the southern border brings Ohio and Kentucky together.

Man made borders on the west and north separate Ohio from Indiana and Michigan.

EARLY DWELLERS

The earliest people who roamed what is now Ohio left very few signs of their presence. Better traces of prehistoric life were left by a group known as the Archaic people; they lived about six or seven thousand years ago.

In 1901 when workmen were digging at the estate called Adena, they found a log tomb of people who lived there perhaps 2,000 years ago. Archeologists called them the Adena people.

Ohio gave another name to an even more interesting prehistoric group who had raised some mounds on the farm of a Mr. Hopewell. The traces of these Hopewell people have been found very widely elsewhere as well as in Ohio.

Archeologists believe the Hopewell people were quite advanced in many ways. This is indicated by a number of kinds of items found in the numerous burial mounds and other mounds they constructed.

Apparently they carried on trade with distant peoples—bringing in copper from Upper Michigan, obsidian from the Rocky Mountains, shells and alligator teeth from the Gulf of Mexico and even items from Aztec or other lands farther south.

One of their best known mounds is an effigy mound laid out like a snake, known as a serpent mound. Fort Ancient State Memorial preserves some of the best examples of Hopewell culture.

Altogether, Ohio's prehistoric past is represented by more than 10,000 mounds of various kinds and periods.

Some mounds were built by people later than the Hopewells who did not have as many skills. All these peoples had vanished before European explorers reached the area.

When early Europeans came into Ohio, a group of Indians known as the

Hopewell culture as shown in a museum diorama

Erie lived in parts of the north. They were driven out by the Iroquois. Their name is remembered in the name of the great lake and the city of Erie, Pennsylvania.

At the time of early exploration, in all of what is now Ohio, experts feel that there were no more than 15,000 Indians, and most of them did not have permanent homes there. Wandering groups came in to hunt and fish.

At a later time other Indian groups were driven out of the east. Portions of Huron, Miami, Delaware and Shawnee tribes then settled in present Ohio.

There may have been European explorers earlier, but history records that Robert Cavelier, Sieur de La Salle, known as La Salle, was the first to reach the area now known as Ohio. This was in his famous exploration in 1669-70.

Because of La Salle's visit, the French claimed the region for themselves. The English also claimed the land and began to send their own men into the region.

George Croghan, Conrad Weiser and Andrew Montour were dispatched to Ohio, attempting to win the friendship of the Indians for the English by giving them trinkets and other gifts.

Croghan found that he could trade many manufactured products available in the east to the Indians in exchange for furs and other valuable items. He became known as "King of the Traders."

To strengthen their claim, the French sent Celeron de Bienville to explore the Ohio River Valley. The Indians must have been surprised by this party of 250 men. They could have been even more surprised by the strange thing the party was doing.

Celeron brought with him a supply of lead plates, stamped with the French claim of ownership. These he buried at six places. The French hoped this would help to prove their ownership of the area. Disregarding the French claims, the British government proposed to give the Ohio Company of Virginia 200,000 acres of Ohio land if they could settle 100 families on the land within seven years.

On October 31, 1750, Christopher Gist was sent from New England to explore the Ohio Company claim. He had made his dog stay home, but, as an interesting sidelight, a day later Gist found that the dog had followed him, and they continued as a party of two.

Gist and his dog spent Christmas at the trading post that George Croghan had established at a Wyandot village.

With the village snowbound on that

THAT'S CURIOUS:
A part of one of the Celeron claim plates ended up in a Massachusetts museum. It had been found by some small boys. Some of it had been melted down for lead bullets but a precious portion had been saved.

Christmas day, Gist read the Bible's Christmas story to the Indians. They listened to their interpreter with great attention.

Before that time the Indians had been suspicious, but by the time Gist left the area the Wyandot had agreed to deal only with the British, and they sent recommendations of Gist to other Indian groups.

Gist was also successful with the Shawnee and Miami. By the time he returned to the east, Gist and his dog had journeyed over and explored much of the land north and west of the Ohio River in what is now Ohio.

His description is interesting: "The Ohio Country is fine, rich, level land, well-timbered with large walnut, ash, sugar trees,...It is well watered...and full of beautiful natural meadows, covered with wild rye, blue grass and clover, and abounds with turkeys, deer, elk and most sorts of game, particularly buffaloes...In short, it wants nothing but cultivation to make it a most delightful country."

The contest between the French and English turned into open war. George Washington was sent to build a fort, which he called Fort Necessity because of the necessity to build it. Before he finished his work the French and Indians attacked, and for the first and only time in his life Washington surrendered.

To punish the Indians for dealing with the British, the French destroyed the Miami village of Pickawillany.

However, the French efforts were not effective, and they gave up their entire mainland North American claims in 1763.

EARLY GROWTH

The British tried to establish the lands west of the mountains as Indian territory, but settlers came in spite of the law.

The great Chief Pontiac led an uprising against the settlers; hundreds were massacred or taken prisoner.

When Colonel Henry Bouquet arrived with an army of 1,500 men, the Indians agreed to settle. They signed a peace agreement at Coshocton in 1764, and returned their prisoners. A few of the smaller children had forgotten their white families and cried at being taken from the Indians.

Subsequently, neither side kept the peace. Finally, in 1774, Virginia Governor Lord Dunmore led an army of 2,500 into the area in an action known as Lord Dunmore's War. The Indians under Chief Cornstalk were beaten.

Under another leader, Chief Logan, the Indians signed a treaty of peace beneath a great tree called "Logan's Elm."

During the Revolution no great battles took place in Ohio. However, British Governor Henry Hamilton became known as the "Hair Buyer" because he offered bounties to the Indians for American scalps. Because of this there was terrible injustice on both sides.

With the American victory, the new nation claimed the lands to the west and northwest.

The new country made a fateful decision about what to do with their new "colonies" on the frontier. They decided that the colonies should be given every chance to become states in their own right. All the provisions for this were contained in the Northwest Ordinance of 1787.

Because of its wise and generous terms, this law has been called the "Magna Charta of the Northwest."

Both Virginia and Connecticut had claimed parts of Ohio. They finally agreed to give up their claims.

If Connecticut had been allowed to keep its claim to Ohio, Cleveland would now be part of Connecticut.

Virginia kept title to nearly 5,000,000 acres, and Connecticut "reserved" another 3,250,000 acres, including the site of Cleveland, and this is still known as the "Western Reserve." The reserved lands were given to the Revolutionary War veterans and others with war claims.

The Ohio Company of Associates was formed in New England in 1787 and sent their first group of 47 settlers to Ohio in the next year.

Reaching the Ohio River, they built two large flatboats; one looked "like a barn on a raft," and floated down the river.

The settlers had been carefully chosen for their ability to build a new town, which they called Marietta. Soon the town was thriving.

Another group floated down that same year and settled on the spot that later became Cincinnati. In spite of Indians and river pirates, more than 10,000 others followed them to Ohio within 12 months.

Once again the Indians were alarmed at the prospect of losing their land. Still encouraged by the British, they killed 900 American soldiers in an ambush, one of the country's worst defeats in battle.

Sent by President Washington, General "Mad Anthony" Wayne built Fort Recovery on the site of the defeat. He also built Fort Defiance and decisively defeated the Indians in the Battle of Fallen Timbers in which the largest Indian army ever assembled fought.

In 1794 the Indians signed the Treaty of Green Ville (Greenville) giving up much of their land claims.

Ohio became a state in 1803. In less than 15 years the population had grown amazingly to more than 70,000.

In the War of 1812, the great Chief Tecumseh took the British side. The Americans won the battle of Fort Meigs and lost the Battle of Raisin River, where Americans were massacred in spite of Tecumseh's efforts. The Americans won again in the Battle of Fort Stephanson, one of the major encounters of the war.

Another major encounter took place on Lake Erie, where Captain Oliver Hazard Perry defeated the British at Put-in-Bay. This is considered one of the major battles of world history because it gave Americans control of the Great Lakes and all of the land they claimed around them.

THAT'S CURIOUS:
Ohio did not become admitted formally as a state until its 150th anniversary in 1953. Someone discovered that Congress had never approved Ohio statehood. This was quickly done and became retroactive to 1803.

The Battle of Lake Erie, as painted by William Powell

In winning this battle, Captain Perry made his famous declaration: "We have met the enemy, and they are ours!"

In one of the Indian treaties the Indians called Colonel Ebenezer Sproat "Hetuck" because he was very tall like the buckeye tree. Hetuck is the Indian word for the buckeye. This was probably the first use of the term "Buckeye" in the sense of a person or persons.

A MIDDLE PERIOD

With the coming of the first steamboat in 1811, river traffic grew rapidly, and Cincinnati became the Queen City of the West. The longest part of the new National Road (now U.S. Highway 40) ran through Ohio, bringing more people and commerce.

In 1816 the capital was moved to its present site at Columbus.

Coming of "Walk-in-the-Water" in 1818, the first steamboat on Lake Erie, and the opening of the Erie Canal in New York provided an easy route to Ohio's Erie lakeshore, and encouraged the great development there.

Two religious groups came to Ohio. Zoar was founded in 1817 by a German group seeking religious freedom. Formed as a communal group they lasted until 1898. The Mormons under Joseph Smith arrived in 1831, prospered and then were driven out seven years later.

The dispute between Ohio and Michigan over territory to the west and south of Toledo almost grew into a real war, but it was settled in Ohio's favor. The dispute was called the Border War.

In the much larger dispute over slavery, many Ohioans helped the cause of the slaves. When author Harriet

President McKinley reviewing troops during the Spanish-American War, painting by G.W. Peters

Beecher Stowe lived in Ohio, she heard the story of a slave woman who escaped with her child across the Ohio River on the ice and wrote her famous "Uncle Tom's Cabin" including the story.

Ohio towns suffered many raids during the war, the northernmost attacks of the conflict.

UP-TO-DATE

More peaceful events followed.

In 1866 the Cincinnati Reds became the first major league baseball team. They won every game their first season. Three years later, also in Cincinnati, the world's first public weather service was made available.

In 1870 John D. Rockefeller laid the foundation for the world's first billion-dollar fortune when he founded the Standard Oil Company in Cleveland. Other new ideas came thick and fast, including Ritty's cash register, the Wrights' early airplane experiments, Kettering's self starter and Brush's storage battery, all products of Ohio inventors.

In 1888 Cincinnati celebrated its Centennial with a great exposition.

The Conservancy Act of 1914 resulted in a series of dams on the Ohio River watershed to help control floods.

The next decades brought difficulties and tragedies—World War I, the Great Depression and, in 1937, the worst Ohio River flood known up to that time.

In World War II 840,000 Ohioans saw service, as hosts of others did in the wars that followed.

Happier days came with the opening

104

of the St. Lawrence Seaway in 1959, bringing deep-sea ships to Ohio Great Lakes ports.

Even more exciting was the exploit of Ohio Astronaut, Neil Armstrong, when he became the first man to set foot on the moon.

Another astronaut, John Glenn, gained a different kind of fame when in 1974 he was elected to the U.S. Senate from Ohio. In 1984 he lost his bid to become the Democratic nominee for president, and President Reagan was a strong winner of Ohio's votes in the 1984 election.

PERSONALITIES

Eight U.S. presidents have been associated with Ohio. Four of the Ohio presidents also were Civil War generals.

Best known of those generals was Ulysses Simpson Grant, whose wartime successes brought him to the White House.

U.S. Grant was not born with those initials. His real name was Hiram Ulysses Grant. His West Point sponsor made the mistake of using Grant's mother's maiden name for her son's middle name, and from that time on he was Ulysses Simpson Grant. After Grant went on to West Point he was not an Ohio resident.

Three of Ohio's generals immediately followed one another in the presidency. Grant was followed by Rutherford B. Hayes, in turn succeeded by James A. Garfield.

Before Hayes became a general, he

PEOPLES

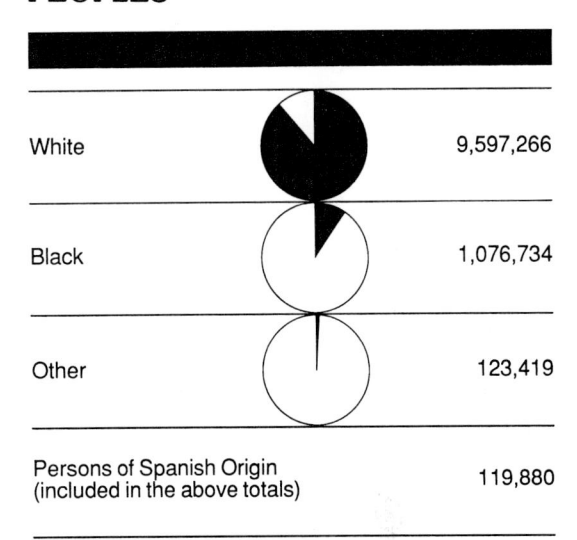

White	9,597,266
Black	1,076,734
Other	123,419
Persons of Spanish Origin (included in the above totals)	119,880

practiced law at Fremont. While serving in the army, he was elected to Congress but would not leave his army post until after the war. His election as president was a real cliff-hanger.

Hayes thought he had lost the election of 1876 to Samuel J. Tilden, but the matter was in dispute. Congress appointed a commission to decide, and they awarded the contested votes to Hayes. The decision was not made until three days before the inauguration on March 5, 1877.

Hayes faithfully kept a diary of every day's activities, and this is one of the most interesting presidential documents. It is now part of the Hayes Memorial at Fremont.

THAT'S CURIOUS:
Harry M. Stevens of Niles decided to make a sandwich of a weiner within a bun; in 1900 when he saw a cartoon showing a dachshound dog made from a weiner, he called his new sandwich invention a "hot dog," and the term stuck.

A native of Orange, James Abram Garfield was a successful general and Congressman before becoming President in January, 1881. Before the year was over he fell to an assassin's bullet, victim of a mentally deranged man.

Of the sad toll of seven U.S. presidents who died in office, four have been from Ohio.

William McKinley, native of Niles, has been a much neglected President. James Wilson, his Secretary of Agriculture, who also served under both Theodore Roosevelt and Taft, declared McKinley was the most able, dedicated and effective of the three presidents.

McKinley has been particularly criticized for his role in the Spanish-American War and for his policies concerning the Spanish territories which came under U.S. control. However, he laid the foundation for the treatment of those territories which kept the U.S. out of the role of a colonial power.

On a trip to Buffalo World's Fair, he stood in a reception line. As he greeted a man wearing a bandage, he was shot by a gun under that bandage. He died less than a week later.

The fourth of Ohio's presidents to die in office was Warren Gamaliel Harding, born near Blooming Grove. His presidency was rocked by scandal and charges of ineptitude. He died at San Francisco after a long illness.

The non-native president associated with Ohio, William Henry Harrison, was the first president to die in office. The hero of Indian fighting in the Ohio area, he served in the U.S. House and Senate and went on to win the presidency. He caught pneumonia during his inauguration and died on April 4, 1841.

His grandson Benjamin Harrison was a native of North Bend. He was another of Ohio's Civil War generals and was Governor of Indiana and U.S. Senator from that state before becoming president in 1888. In 1892 he was defeated in his reelection bid.

William Howard Taft was a native of Cincinnati. His father had been a well-known public figure before him. The son served as civil governor of the Philippines and provisional governor of Cuba and was T. Roosevelt's Secretary of War.

As Roosevelt's protege, Taft won the presidency in 1908. He was the only man in history to serve both as president and as Chief Justice of the United States. His son Robert Taft was one of Ohio's best known senators.

Among other public figures, Ohio contributed 51 commanding generals in the Civil War, including dynamic William Tecumseh Sherman, native of Lancaster, and Philip H. Sheridan of Somerset.

Some of the greatest inventions came from the minds of Ohio men, including Thomas A. Edison, native of Milan.

Much of the pioneer aviation work of the Wright Brothers was done in their shop at Dayton.

Inventor Charles Kettering, with his electric starter, James Rutty with his cash register, and Charles Martin Hall with his aluminum processing method, all were Ohioans.

A black writer is Ohio's most famous

THAT'S CURIOUS:
James Ritty called his first cash register a "Mechanical Money Drawer."

poet. Paul Laurence Dunbar of Dayton grew up in poverty. He received much encouragement from his mother and from Central High School at Dayton, where he was encouraged in his writing. Before he died at the age of 34, he had published seven volumes of poetry, two volumes of short stories and two novels.

It is possible that another Ohio author ranks second only to the Bible in the number of books distributed. He is William Holmes McGuffey. Dr. McGuffey was a prominent educator, President of Ohio University at Athens. However, he was best known as the author of a series of books called McGuffey Readers. His reading texts were used almost exclusively by many generations of learners. They have never been out of print and are again growing ever more popular.

Another Ohio author, Zane Grey of the important Zane family of Zanesville, was an author of western novels whose works also have sold in the multi-millions.

Famed Ohio composers include Daniel Emmett who composed "Dixie."

An almost legendary Ohio figure was Jonathan Chapman, known as Johnny Appleseed. He wandered around Ohio and the adjoining states planting apple seeds, and becoming a beloved figure wherever he went. Some of the plantings have been perpetuated to the present time.

USING THE NATURAL WEALTH

Only three other states surpass Ohio in wealth from manufacturing.

Several Ohio cities are world centers of their industries.

The leadership of Akron in rubber products was started when Dr. Benjamin

Paul Laurence Dunbar is honored by a U.S. stamp

Franklin Goodrich produced the first successful vulcanized rubber fire hose, then went on to tires. From this start came the huge company that bears his name. Other large rubber companies followed.

East Cleveland became the site of the enormous General Electric company formed from the companies of Thomas A. Edison and Charles F. Brush. As early as 1900, Cleveland was the center for automobile manufacturing. More than 80 different names were attached to autos made in Cleveland. Charles B. Shanks, Cleveland newspaperman, is given credit for coining the word "automobile" itself.

The city is still a leading producer of auto body parts, glass and accessories.

With its mammoth factories turning out cleansing materials of all kinds,

107

THAT'S CURIOUS:
When a Cincinnati worker made a mistake in the soap he was mixing, air bubbles were trapped in the product. The mistake was not discovered; the soap was shipped, and orders began to come in for the soap that floated. Ivory Soap had just been accidentally invented.

Cincinnati still ranks as one of the leaders in soap and related products.

Other "name" centers for products are Toledo for the Jeep and scales, and Canton for vacuum cleaners.

Once the leading state in corn production, Ohio still produces corn and popcorn along with soybeans, cattle and dairy products.

The state is renowned for the vast acreage where fruits, flowers and vegetables are grown under glass in greenhouses.

Altogether, Ohio ranks fifth in agricultural income.

THE ECONOMY

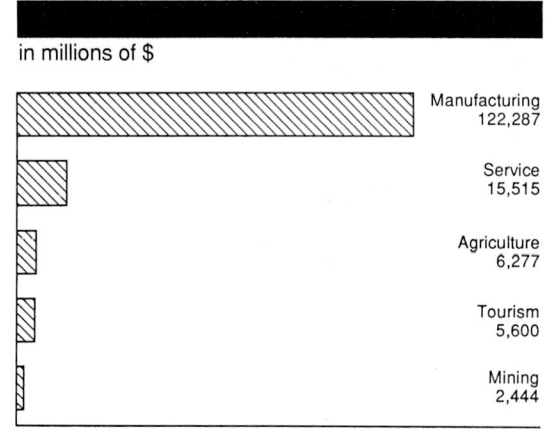

in millions of $

Manufacturing 122,287
Service 15,515
Agriculture 6,277
Tourism 5,600
Mining 2,444

Principal Products:
   machinery and electrical equipment, transportation equipment
Agriculture:
   dairy products, soybeans, corn, cattle, greenhouse products

From its plentiful reserves, Ohio still produces more than 30 million tons of coal annually. Oil and gas reserves remain large and continue to produce revenue for the state.

Great resources of sandstone and limestone are worked. Near Barberton is the deepest limestone mine in the world, and the world's largest sandstone quarry is worked at South Amherst.

Ohio ranks number one in the manufacture of clay products, due to the large supplies of some of the world's finest clays.

All the salt needs of the U.S. for the next 150,000 years could be produced from Ohio's salt reserves, and the state ranks high in salt production.

GETTING AROUND

As a principal producer and nourisher of U.S. presidents, Ohio takes special pride in preserving their memories and making available to tourists the related sites.

Beginning a tour of presidential sites in the area of Cincinnati, at North Bend the visitors see the William Henry Harrison tomb, a state memorial.

Point Pleasant has restored the one-room home of President Grant.

At Cincinnati is the Taft National Historic Site.

Rutherford B. Hayes Library and Museum State Memorial at Fremont is situated on a beautiful 25-acre estate.

The restored Harding home is at Marion.

Lawnfield is the 26-room home at Mentor of James A. Garfield.

Mc Kinley Birthplace National Memorial at Niles is a splendid marble structure honoring the martyred President.

The ancient peoples are remembered in their many mounds, including Serpent Mound State Memorial, Peebles, where the coiled earthen snake appears to be swallowing a huge earthen egg.

Ohio's largest city was founded by Moses Cleaveland in 1796, and a printer changed the spelling to Cleveland to fit his page.

Heart of Ohio's largest city is Public Square. Other attractions are the Cleveland Symphony, one of the country's best; the Cleveland Health Museum, pioneer of its type; and Cultural Gardens in Rockefeller Park, unique in its field.

At Columbus, the grand capitol building belies its modern look, having been started in 1839. However, it was not completed until 1861. This required the work of five different architects under 12 governors.

Cincinnati maintains its reputation as a center of American culture, a culture which developed amazingly from the earliest days.

Some of the world's top musicians have been trained in and worked in Cincinnati. They helped to create one of the top symphony orchestras. In addition to its regular season, the Cincinnati Symphony plays a popular summer series at Riverbend Music Center.

The Cincinnati Zoo, Museum of

Cleveland

Natural History, and Cincinnati Art Museum represent other cultural and scientific areas in which the city excels.

Riverfront Stadium is home of the first professional baseball team, the Cincinnati Reds, as well as football's Cincinnati Bengals.

COMPAC-FACS
OHIO
Buckeye State

HISTORY
Statehood: March 1, 1803
Admitted as: 17th state
Capital: Columbus
OFFICIAL SYMBOLS
Motto: With God, All Things Are Possible
Bird: Cardinal

THAT'S CURIOUS:
Two unusual structures are the "House That Jack (a mule) Built," at Bellaire and the unusual three-ended bridge at Zanesville.

The Ohio capitol

Insect: Ladybug
Flower: Scarlet carnation
Tree: Buckeye
Beverage: Tomato Juice
Gem: Ohio flint
Song: "Beautiful Ohio"
GEO-FACS
Area: 41,004 sq. mi.
Rank in Area: 35th
Length (n/s): 210 mi.
Width (e/w): 230 mi.
Geographic Center: 25 mi. nne of Columbus in Delaware Co.
Highest Point: 1,550 ft. (Campbell Hill)
Lowest Point: 473 ft. (Ohio River)
Mean Elevation: 850 ft.
Temperature, Extreme Range: 152 degrees
Number of Counties: 88
POPULATION
Total: 10,746,000 (1983)
Rank: 6th
Density: 262 persons per sq. mi.
Principal Cities: Cleveland, 573,822; Columbus, 565,032; Cincinnati, 385,457; Toledo, 354,635; Akron, 237,177; Dayton, 203,371; Youngstown, 115,436
EDUCATION
Schools: 4,826, elementary and secondary
Higher: 135
VITAL STATISTICS
Births (1980/83): 541,000
Deaths (1980/83): 314,000
Hospitals: 237
Drinking Age: 19/21 (limited purchase at 19)
INTERESTING PEOPLE
William Henry Harrison, Benjamin Harrison, Ulysses Simpson Grant, Rutherford B. Hayes, James Abram Garfield, William Mc Kinley, Warren Gamaliel Harding, William Howard Taft, Robert A. Taft, William Tecumseh Sherman, Philip Sheridan, Thomas A. Edison, Orville Wright, Wilbur Wright, Paul Laurence Dunbar, William Holmes McGuffey, Zane Grey, Jonathan (Johnny Appleseed) Chapman, Neil Armstrong, John Brown, Clark Gable, Charles M. Hall, Bob Hope, Pete Rose, Roy Rogers, Harriet Beecher Stowe
WHEN DID IT HAPPEN?
1670: La Salle explores
1750: Christopher Gist explores
1763: England wins the area from France
1787: Area under Northwest Territory
1788: Marietta is first settlement, Cincinnati founded
1795: Indian Wars end with Treaty of Green Ville
1796: Cleveland founded
1803: Statehood
1811: First steamboat arrives
1813: Put-in-Bay, Perry Victory
1816: Columbus supersedes Chillicothe as capital
1836: Border War settled
1840: W. H. Harrison elected president
1868: U.S. Grant elected president
1877: Rutherford B. Hayes elected president
1896: William McKinley elected president
1980: William Howard Taft elected president
1913: Great flood
1920: W. G. Harding elected president
1937: Greatest Ohio River flood up to that time
1955: Ohio Turnpike dedicated
1959: Opening of St. Lawrence Seaway
1969: Neil Armstrong steps on moon
1974: John Glenn elected to Senate
1984: Glenn loses presidential nomination attempt

WISCONSIN

FASCINATING WISCONSIN

This account of Wisconsin is being written on Mark Twain's "Literary Piano," invented by a Wisconsin man.

That is just one of the many fascinating facts to be recounted in the story of Wisconsin.

These include the dog prairie, the left-handed mittenland, Paul Bunyan's big splash and the 150-foot man.

Among people associated with the state are a "Chinese" explorer, the burrowing miners, the eaters of wild rice and the man who swore in trees as official witnesses.

Wisconsin is the state with the most famous of all our national symbols, a bald eagle once caged in the state capitol. That capitol has no cornerstone and was never officially dedicated.

These are just a few of the true stories which spice the reading about the great state of Wisconsin.

THE FACE OF WISCONSIN

In the Indian language the word "Wisconsin" means "the gathering of the waters." Those waters have always been very important in the state's history and economy.

Several rivers and two Great Lakes make up considerably more than half of Wisconsin's boundaries. Within those boundaries are more than 10,000 rivers and streams and nearly 9,000 lakes.

The Mississippi River on the west and the St. Croix on the northwest form most of the western border. On the northeast are the Brule and Menominee river borders.

Balance Rock, one of Wisconsin's unusual geological formations

The eastern border is entirely formed by Lake Michigan, including Green Bay, the second largest bay on the Great Lakes.

On the map the shape of Wisconsin is roughly like a left-handed mitten. The peninsula of Door County forms the thumb. Stretching out from the Thumb are Washington Island and other smaller islands.

Another splendid inlet, Chequamegon Bay, indents the state's Lake Superior shoreline. It too has its cluster of islands, known as the Apostles.

At Wisconsin's northeast corner, the state shares with Minnesota one of the busiest inland ports in the world—the Superior-Duluth harbor.

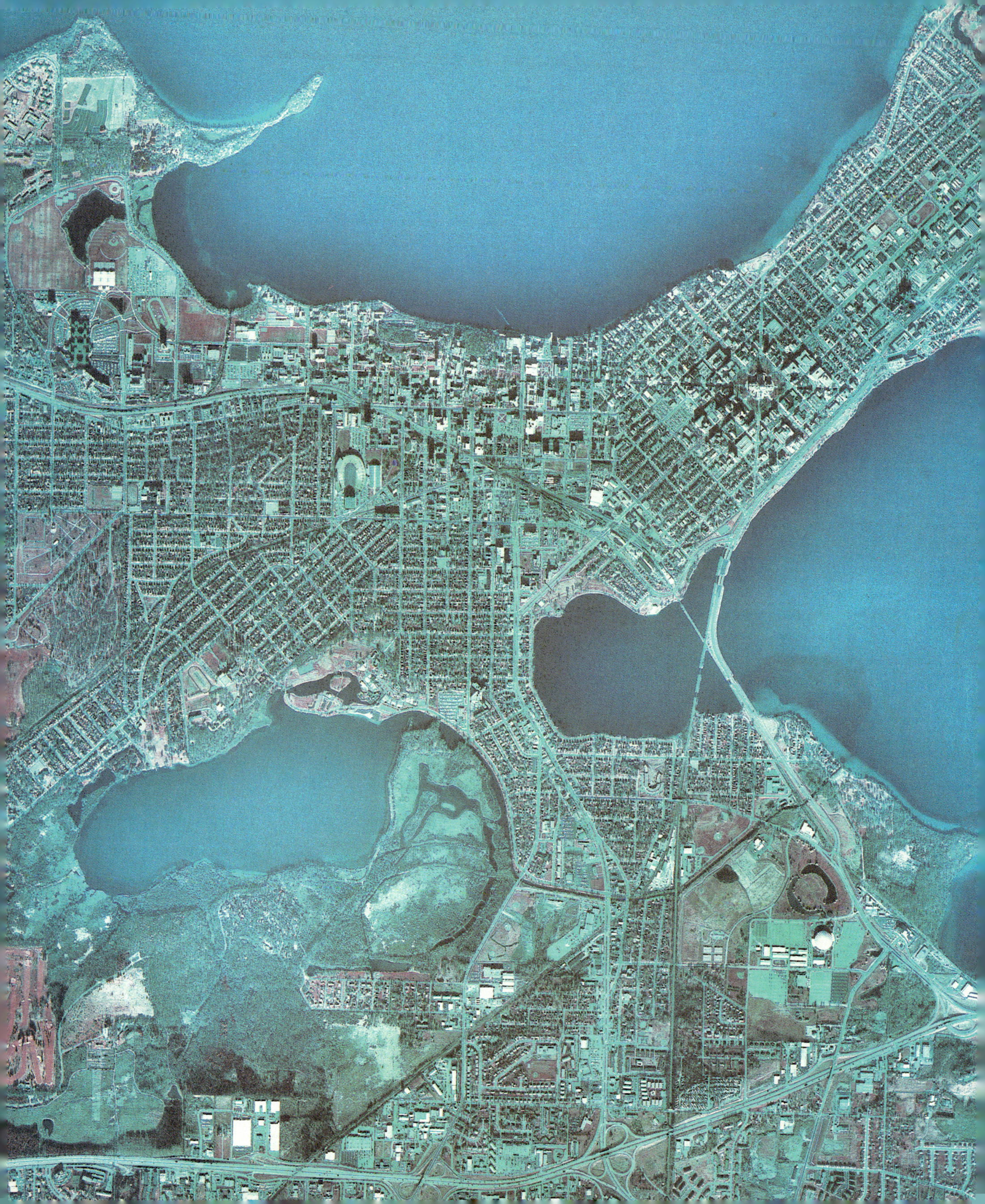

THAT'S CURIOUS:
Wisconsin people have a story about how the lakes were formed. They say the giant mythical lumberman Paul Bunyan jumped off Rib Mountain into the Wisconsin River, and the water he splashed up created the sparkling lakes.

In addition to Minnesota, the neighboring states are Iowa, Illinois and Michigan.

Wisconsin's inland rivers have been particularly useful. The map shows clearly that the Fox River flowing through Green Bay into Lake Michigan and the Wisconsin River emptying into the Mississippi almost come together near Portage.

This means that the water route from the Great Lakes to the Mississippi was separated by only about 1 1/2 miles of land. Using this route, travelers to the region could carry their canoes across the short portage and avoid the hundreds of weary miles of tramping overland.

Other major Wisconsin rivers include the Roc, Black, Flambeau and Chippewa.

The largest of the many inland lakes is Lake Winnebago.

The surface of Wisconsin today is much as it was when the last of the four great glaciers melted away to the north.

Standing in the path of the glaciers was tough, very old Rib Mountain. This old giant forced the glaciers to split and move to either side, leaving large parts of present southern Wisconsin free of glacier forces. This is known as unglaciated or "driftless" area.

In the rest of the state, the glaciers leveled hills, filled in valleys, and gouged out holes. These holes or basins filled with water and eventually became many of the lakes known today.

(Opposite) Madison as seen from on high by NHAP/EROS

EARLY DWELLERS

Baraboo is known for its circus life. However, the 150-foot "man" found near there was never part of any circus.

This man-shape was formed by prehistoric peoples who piled up earth in human form. Many of these "effigy" mounds have been found in the state. They take many forms—turtles, snakes and other figures.

Other kinds of mounds have been found, some piled up with no special form like small hills. These were simply refuse piles where junk was heaped up over the years; others were for burials. The bodies and other items found in the mounds tell a good many things about the people who made them.

Even earlier than the mound builders, probably about 8,000 B.C., other peoples lived in the Wisconsin area. These Copper Culture people knew how to pound and hammer copper into jewelry and other items. Near Oconto one of their burial grounds was unearthed.

Perhaps most interesting of all the prehistoric peoples known to have been in the Wisconsin area were the people who lived in a town now called Aztalan. It took this name because some experts feel it was founded by the Aztec people from Mexico.

If this is the case, Aztalan is the most northerly point thought to have been settled by the Aztecs.

These people were more skilled than

Milwaukee Public Museum's display pictures Aztalan as it might have looked in 1200 A.D.

their neighbors in many ways, such as working with shell, antler, bone, and stone as well as copper.

However, the Aztalans apparently hunted other people for food. Their village was burned, probably by vengeful neighbors.

It is strange to realize that these cannibal people from far to the south were probably there within a hundred years of the first European explorations.

At that time dwellers in the area were the Winnebago, a Sioux-related group. They were joined by Algonquin tribes, driven into Wisconsin from the east.

Among the most important of the Algonquin groups was the Menominee tribe. Their name means eaters of wild rice. The rice harvest was one of their important sources of food.

One of their best-known chiefs was Oshkosh, for whom the city is named. His descendants and other Menominee still live on their lands in Wisconsin.

An interesting Menominee custom concerned their wedding ceremony. The bride and groom exchanged blankets. A dissatisfied partner could return the blanket and dissolve the marriage.

STIRRINGS

One of the most dramatic events in American exploration occurred in 1634 at Red Banks near Green Bay.

The Indians on the bank watched in awe as a figure stepped from a canoe. This was Jean Nicolet, dressed in long gorgeous robes and a hat with waving plumes, as he thought the people of China would dress. He thought he might have reached China's shores.

He raised the two curved "sticks" in his hand, and fire and smoke and a loud noise came from them. The Indians were paralyzed with fear.

Obviously the Indians were not Chinese, but Nicolet had been sent from French Canada not only to find the route to China, which had been sought for so long, but also to make friends with the Indians. He was the first European known to have been in present Wisconsin.

Early French fur traders de Groseilliers and Radisson were followed by other traders as well as missionaries called "Black Robes." Among these latter were Father Rene Menard and Father Claude Allouez, who founded the Mission of St. Francis Xavier at Oconto.

One of the missionaries was Father Jacques Marquette. With Louis Jolliet he left Green Bay, paddled by canoe up the Fox River, crossed the portage into the Wisconsin River and floated down that stream to its mouth where they discovered the upper Mississippi in 1673, "with a joy that I cannot express," as Father Marquette wrote.

Both the French and British claimed the area, but in 1763 the French gave up their claims.

A year later, Green Bay became the first permanent European settlement in what is now Wisconsin. In 1781 Prairie du Chien was founded on the Mississippi.

After the American Revolution, the British agreed to give up their hold on the area. In spite of this they continued to hold much of the region. The War of 1812 ended their resistance.

Wisconsin's only major part in the War of 1812 concerned the burning of Fort McKay by the British in 1813. It was built for the protection of Prairie du Chien.

EARLY GROWTH

Wisconsin had been organized as part of the Northwest Territory. Later it was in turn part of Indiana, Illinois, Michigan and Wisconsin territories.

Southwestern Wisconsin was the scene of a growing mineral rush to work the valuable lead deposits there. The area became a rip-roaring frontier, much like those farther west at a later time, with gang brawls and gunfights, high-stake poker games and other familiar sounding activities.

There was so little time for the miners to build houses that they sometimes burrowed into hillsides like badgers, and before long they took the nickname "Badgers," which has stuck ever since.

Mineral Point was established as a county seat in 1829-30, and there were 1,500 settlers in the area.

In 1832 Chief Black Hawk tried to regain tribal lands in Illinois. When Federal troops resisted, the struggle was known as the Black Hawk War.

Pushed into Wisconsin, the Chief tried to surrender at the so-called Battle of Bad Axe, but many of his people were shot or drowned as they tried to cross to the Iowa side of the Mississippi, and the Indians suffered their final defeat.

THAT'S CURIOUS:
The St. Francis chapel burned, but the beautiful silver monstrance was discovered more than 100 years after the fire and is a prized exhibit at the Neville Museum, Green Bay.

Milwaukee's founders would not know the city today

Wisconsin Territory included much more land than present Wisconsin. To govern the entire region a new capital was chosen and begun. It was named Madison.

Milwaukee was incorporated in 1846. The Wisconsin population shot up by more than 200,000, and statehood came in 1848.

The population continued to swell; so many immigrants arrived from German lands that the state became known as a second Germany. Many Scandinavians and Swiss also came to make their homes.

On March 20, 1854, a group of politicians met and formed a new party which they named Republican. Other states claim the honor, but Wisconsin believes this was the founding of the national Republican Party. The schoolhouse where the party met is now a historic site.

In a disputed election of 1856, Republicans elected Coles Rashford as Wisconsin Governor.

The state made educational news in 1856 when Mrs. Carl Schurz began the nation's first kindergarten at Watertown.

The disagreement over slavery took a strange turn when an escaped slave, Joshua Glover, living in Racine was captured and taken to a Milwaukee jail by federal marshals.

Before he could be returned to slavery a mob assembled by abolitionist newspaperman Sherman M. Booth set Glover free, and he escaped to Canada. Booth was arrested, set free by the state, arrested by federal officers, again escaped, again arrested and finally pardoned by President Buchanan.

A MIDDLE PERIOD

Because Wisconsin Governor Alexander Randall foresaw the Civil War, his state was rather well prepared for the conflict, and volunteers more than met the draft quota.

Louis P. Harvey, governor in 1862, volunteered to take medical supplies to Wisconsin soldiers wounded in the Battle of Shiloh. His services were very useful, but he fell from a steamboat on the Tennessee River, and the body was never recovered. He had served only 73 days as governor.

His wife, Cordelia Harvey, was primarily responsible for improving the hospital care of wounded Civil War servicemen.

In 1871 the summer had been dry, and the forests were like tinder. On October 8, Peshtigo seemed to burst into flame like an explosion. That fire took 1,200 lives of Wisconsin people, 800 of them from Peshtigo. Some escaped at Peshtigo by lying in the river. One man wrote, "I saw nothing but flames; houses, trees, and the air itself was on fire."

By an extremely strange coincidence, many also died in a Michigan forest fire on the same day. Strangest of all, that was the very day of the much more famous fire which swept most of Chicago, Illinois.

UP-TO-DATE

Wisconsin was the scene of a number of important developments in industry.

Dr. F.W. Carhart had developed a steam automobile as early as 1873. Two years later the state offered a $10,000 prize for development of a better auto, to be awarded to the winner of a race. That race is considered the world's first automobile race. An Oshkosh car won.

An invention which changed the world perhaps as much as the auto was the typewriter, invented by C. Latham Sholes in 1869.

Wisconsin pioneered in producing electricity from water power, with Appleton having the world's first such plant. It may have been the first public generating plant of any type.

In 1901 a new era in politics came to Wisconsin with Robert M. La Follette, first governor to have been born in the state.

At the governor's urging, the state passed the first statewide primary election law in 1904. La Follette and Wisconsin developed social legislation later adopted by many states.

As time went by, laws were passed governing child labor, aid to dependent children, assistance to the aged, pensions for the blind, unemployment compensation and others. This kind of social program came to be known as the Wisconsin Idea.

THAT'S CURIOUS:

One of the most famous mascots of all time was Old Abe of Wisconsin's Eagle Regiment. He went everywhere with his men, took part in parades, stole chickens from the company cook and took part in 42 battles. After the war Abe lived in a cage in the capitol at Madison. Ironically, after surviving so many battles, Abe died in a capitol fire. He was stuffed and displayed in a museum until that too was destroyed by fire. Today another stuffed eagle represents Abe in the capitol.

Robert M. La Follette by Chester La Follette

La Follette's party was called the Progressive Republican Party.

La Follette went on to the U.S. Senate where he opposed U.S. entry into World War I. He voted against the war declaration but later supported the war effort.

With the country at war with Germany, the German population faced questions about their loyalty. However, there proved to be little difficulty on that point, and 125,000 men and women from Wisconsin went into military service.

La Follette remained in the Senate until his death in 1925.

The Second World War called 350,000 Wisconsin men and women into service. The state's many industries played an important part in the war effort.

Sports-loving Wisconsinites rejoiced in 1953 when the baseball Braves moved to Milwaukee, and joy was even greater when they won the World Series in 1957.

The Great Lakes seaports of Wisconsin had long been important, but with the 1959 opening of the St. Lawrence Seaway, the ports of the whole world became available on the inland "seas." Milwaukee gave a resounding welcome to British Queen Elizabeth II and Prince Philip, who came to help dedicate the seaway.

Not so happy was the 1961 change in which the Federal Government gave up control of the Menominee Indian Reservation, forming a private company. Heavy taxes and lack of capital hampered the Indian company, and in 1973 Congress voted to return the reservation to federal control.

In the period of 1970-1983, Wisconsin continued to grow with the Midwest's largest percentage of population gain.

PERSONALITIES

Robert Marion La Follette was born at Primrose of a poor family. He worked his way through the University of Wisconsin by teaching in a country school.

As a U.S. Congressman he generally followed the Republican line, but he broke with the party and appealed directly to the people of the state. He failed in bids for the governorship in 1896 and 1898, but won in 1900.

In 1911 he was one of the founders of the Progressive Republican Party, and wanted the party's nomination for president. However, Theodore Roosevelt "stole" most of the Progressive votes from him.

From 1919 until his death in 1925, Robert M. La Follette was one of the most powerful men in the Senate.

His son, Robert M. La Follette, Jr., succeeded him in the Senate in 1925 and served until his defeat in 1947. Another son, Philip Fox La Follette served as Wisconsin's governor.

Wisconsin personalities have given the state an outstanding reputation in science and industry.

Christopher Latham Sholes spent six years and made twenty-five different models before he perfected his typing machine. For a while it did not catch on.

However, famed author Mark Twain bought what he called a "literary piano" which he extolled; the typewriter caused a sensation at the Philadelphia world's fair, and was on its way into almost every office and home.

A Wisconsin man, John Stevens, invented the important rolling mill method for processing flour.

Another Wisconsin man, Allen Lapham, has been credited as the "Father of the United States Weather Service." He knew that farmers, travelers and others could be helped if they had some advance notice of the weather.

At his urging the government established the bureau, with Lapham as assistant director. The first forecast proved to be correct, although some cynics say it has not been right since.

John Appleby produced a device which greatly reduced labor on the farm. He perfected a machine to tie bundles of grain; this previously could only be done by hand.

Almost every sportsman knows the name Evinrude, although many may not know the man behind the name. Ole Evinrude invented and manufactured the outboard motor for boats.

William Hoard devoted his life to improving the dairy industry and has been called the father of modern dairying.

PEOPLES

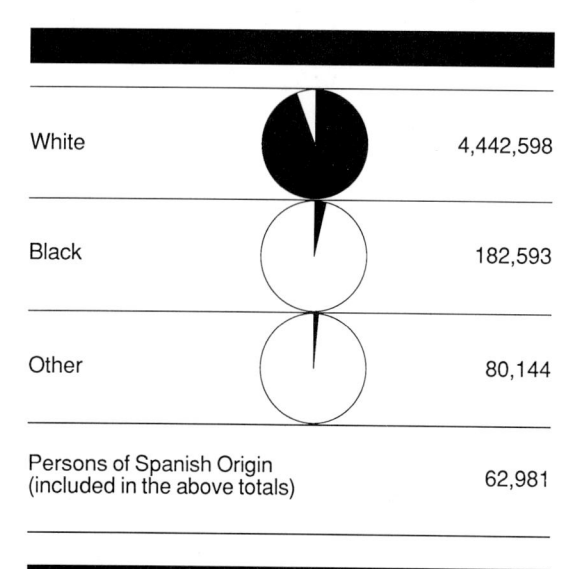

White		4,442,598
Black		182,593
Other		80,144
Persons of Spanish Origin (included in the above totals)		62,981

Perhaps even more important was Dr. Stephen M. Babcock's discovery of the method of testing milk for butterfat. This has been called one of the great discoveries of modern times. Dr. Babcock did not patent his discovery and gave it freely for worldwide use.

Dr. Babcock went on to make perhaps an even more important discovery—that of vitamins and their role.

Dr. William Beaumont also advanced health knowledge with his famous studies of digestive processes, using a human subject.

Few people in modern history outside of politics have become so well known and so controversial as a Richland Center native, Frank Lloyd Wright.

Hailed by many as one of the leading

119

architects of all time, Wright was also much criticized for being too far out and for the unusual shapes and ideas he introduced into architecture and furniture. Some of his most important contributions were in working out new methods of construction and the use of new materials.

His home at Spring Green, called Taliesin, became a center for the study of architecture by some of the young architects who also gained fame later.

One of Wright's best known buildings was one of his last—the spiral Guggenheim Museum of Art in New York City.

Vinnie Ream, native of Madison, became one of the best-known sculptors. She was the first woman to be commissioned by Congress to create a sculpture—the famed statue of Lincoln in the capitol at Washington.

Other creative Wisconsinites were writers Hamlin Garland, Ben Hecht, and Edna Ferber, and composer Carrie Jacobs Bond.

A WEALTH OF NATURE

In pioneer days almost all of Wisconsin was covered with the most beautiful primeval forests. Wisconsin still has 15,000,000 acres of forest land, including the knot-free, tall and straight white pine.

The forests were home to a wide variety of wildlife, including the incredible flocks of millions of passenger pigeons which sometimes blocked out the sun as they journeyed. Sadly, they are now extinct.

More fortunate is the magnificent whistling swan, now making a comeback. Their migrations are almost as precise as the famous swallows at Capistrano. The swans can be counted on to arrive at Green Bay between March 19 and 23.

Wisconsin is a leader in conservation and its huge game farm at Poynette is said to be the world's largest.

The badger still forages for food at night and burrows into the earth by day, one of nature's fastest diggers. It was this burrowing ability that was imitated by early miners and gave the state its name as the Badger State.

Much of the lead mined in early days is gone, along with the rich iron ores of the Lake Superior region. Some zinc remains, as well as supplies of building stone, sand and gravel. Rib Mountain offers a whole mountain of granite for quarrying.

USING THE WEALTH

Wisconsin has long been proud of its title as the Dairy State. Well it should be, since it has held the leadership in milk and milk products continuously since 1919, accounting for more than 15 percent of the nation's total.

The state has been a leader in cheese making since 1859, when Hiram Smith introduced the industry. Another great favorite after its discovery by inventor William Horlick was malted milk.

THAT'S CURIOUS:
The "Witness Trees" of a Wisconsin man have gone down in American lore. Justice of the Peace Pat Kelly of Hickory sometimes could not find a witness for a wedding due to the small population. He was known to swear in the nearest tree as a witness. It is not quite clear how the tree was able to sign.

In other aspects of agriculture, wild rice was probably the first harvested grain. It is still an Indian favorite, but the supplies are dwindling.

Wisconsin grows more hay and green peas than any other state, along with leading in inland cranberry growing.

The state pioneered in one of the most important modern agricultural methods—contour farming practices.

Women who enjoy fur coats should give a special thanks to Wisconsin. The state leads all others in production of mink pelts at more than 1,500 mink farms. There is still some activity in trapping wild fur-bearing animals.

At the height of Wisconsin's lumbering days, hundreds of millions of board feet were cut and floated down the rivers to market. Sometimes the logs would be tied together in rafts. Occasionally a family would float downriver on one of these for a picnic or just for the joyride.

Wisconsin timber is still important. The world's largest hardwood sawmill operates at Laona, and the country's largest hardwood manufacturing operation is carried on at Algoma.

One of the world's most important timber experiment stations is the U.S. Forest Products Laboratory at Madison, where forest growth, conservation and new products are researched.

Zinc, sand and gravel and building stone are still mined. Particularly important is the unique red granite industry at Wausau.

Because of the large supplies of wood pulp used in making paper, paper making started early in Wisconsin, at the Neenah-Menasha region. Today the state leads all others in producing paper and paper products of the widest variety.

THE ECONOMY

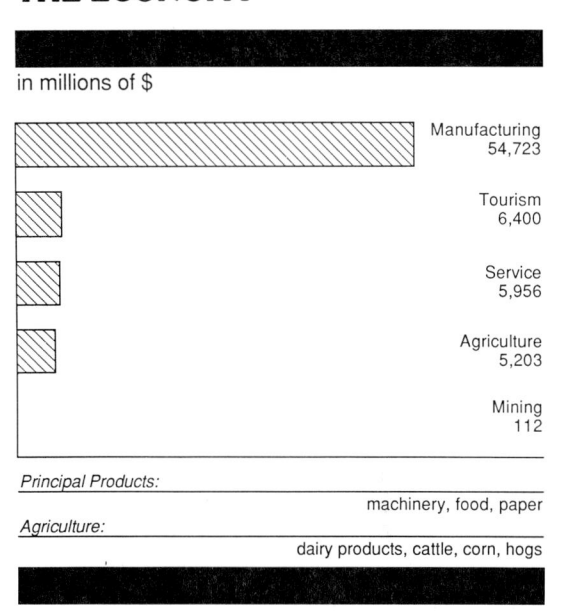

in millions of $

- Manufacturing 54,723
- Tourism 6,400
- Service 5,956
- Agriculture 5,203
- Mining 112

Principal Products: machinery, food, paper

Agriculture: dairy products, cattle, corn, hogs

Research on new methods, new products and solution of problems of the paper industry is carried on at the Institute of Paper Chemistry at Appleton.

Machinery to produce paper is also important in Wisconsin manufacturing. One firm at Beloit produces more than half of the country's machines for making paper. The giant machines they manufacture can turn out a mile of paper in just one minute.

Other heavy machinery has long been produced in Wisconsin. Most of the great steam shovels used in digging the Panama Canal were manufactured in Wisconsin, and the state continues to manufacture some of the largest of this kind of equipment.

In a very different field, Milwaukee has long been known as the "Brewing Capital of the World."

However, equipment used in all the

The unique Wisconsin capitol

phases of electric power leads beer in dollar volume in the city. The city also is a leader in gasoline engines, outboard motors, padlocks and wheelbarrows.

The state pioneered in the production of utensils made of aluminum, and Wisconsin continues to produce these in quantity.

Plumbing fixtures and enamelware are prime industries in the state, with the Kohler Plant at Kohler and Vollrath Company at Sheboygan as leading producers.

GETTING AROUND

The Indians called the Wisconsin area "weesechoseck," meaning a "good place to live" in Menominee language. Today it is not only a good place to live but a great place to visit. Revenue from tourists ranks second only to manufacturing.

The Menominee also had a name for a location on the Lake Michigan shore, which they called malm-a-waukee sape, or gathering place by the river. This of course gave the name to the state's largest city—Milwaukee.

Milwaukee has many attractions. The influence of a large number of German people who settled in the city is still felt, particularly in cooking. Milwaukee boasts some of the finest German restaurants outside Germany itself.

One of the newest and finest natural history museums attracts many visitors to its unusual displays.

The County War Memorial and Art Center and Municipal Pier enhance the lakefront. Mitchell Park Horticultural Conservatory is known worldwide for its dramatic building and the quality of its displays.

Milwaukee's Summerfest is one of the major annual festivals of the country.

West of Milwaukee is the town of Oconomowoc, once the home of very wealthy and powerful people, and still a pleasant community surrounded by lakes.

Even more prominent as the summer home of wealthy families is Lake Geneva, which remains as a magnet for tourists; boat trips around the lovely lake reveal many magnificent homes. Yerkes Observatory on Lake Geneva is an important astronomical resource.

Two handsome lakes dominate the Madison scene. At Madison, the dome of the capitol makes it the second highest capitol in the country.

This is the last of five capitols in various previous capital cities. Designed in the unusual form of a Greek cross, it was finished in 1917. Even more unusual is the fact that there is no record of a cornerstone, and the building was never officially dedicated.

Of great interest is the main campus of the University of Wisconsin at Madison, scenically situated on Lake Mendota. Both academically and athletically, it ranks high among all the state universities.

One of the finest of all state historical societies is the one at Madison. It is especially noted for its fine publications on state, local and regional history.

Madison pioneered in radio broadcasting. Station WHA is the world's oldest station in continual operation. It was also the first educational radio station and the first to broadcast music appreciation programs.

Wisconsin has several small communities which have kept the appearance and traditions of the home countries of the people who settled there. Little Norway was built around the Norway building, which was moved there from the World's Columbian Exposition.

"Swissconsin" is another name for the Village of New Glarus due to the Swiss people who moved there and continued to cherish Swiss customs.

New Glarus holds a notable annual William Tell festival, with a Tell pageant, flag throwers, yodelers, and bell ringers, along with their Alpine horns.

Not far away is the Swiss cheese center of America at Monroe; the Spring Green home of architect Frank Lloyd Wright and the architectural school he founded there are much-visited shrines.

Mineral Point, with its memories of the lead mining boom, is an important historical center, with fine homes and many memories of the Welsh settlers.

Probably one of the most-visited tourist centers in the country is the Wisconsin Dells region. The rocky cliffs and narrow canyons carved by the Wisconsin River are of special interest in the Midwest where such scenery is unusual. The many man-made tourist attractions also bring hosts of visitors to the Dells.

At nearby Baraboo a unique Circus World Museum recalls the days when Wisconsin led the country as a circus center. Many fine old circus wagons and other relics are preserved there. Baraboo was home of the Ringling Brothers who developed the largest of all the circuses.

Green Bay as the oldest permanent Wisconsin settlement and its Tank Cottage, the oldest building still standing, are tourist attractions. No other city of its size has a full-scale professional football team, and the Green Bay Packers are often contenders for leadership.

Sturgeon Bay is the grand entrance to the wonderful resort vacationland of Door County. In Door County one of the many attractions is the noted summer theater and music festival. Nearby Egg Harbor got its name from an egg throwing battle of vacationeers who tossed eggs at one another.

Across the state is Wisconsin's second oldest city—Prairie du Chien, on the Mississippi. The peculiar and unique

THAT'S CURIOUS:
The Ringling Brothers began their circus days as young boys with a menagerie of chickens, rabbits, a billy goat and a horse. While still in their early teens they had developed a circus with tents, pennants and all the trimmings. From this they went on to "The Greatest Show on Earth."

name is French for Prairie of the Dogs. A telling reminder of the wealth of fur trading days at Prairie du Chien is Villa Louis, the mansion built in 1843 by fur trader Hercules Dousman, the state's first millionaire. He built a private racetrack with an imported cork surface, and lived royally in many ways. Visitors may still visit the restored mansion.

La Crosse is another historic Mississippi town. The community sprang up around the spacious la crosse playing fields, a popular Indian game.

Popular attractions of the northwest are Interstate Park near St. Croix Falls, the community of Rhinelander, a gateway to a region of 232 lakes, and the Eagle River chain, longest of its type.

Northernmost parts of Wisconsin are the Apostle Islands, not twelve, as in the Bible, but totalling twenty-three.

COMPAC-FACS
WISCONSIN
Badger State

HISTORY
Statehood: May 29, 1848
Admitted as: 30th state
Capital: Madison
OFFICIAL SYMBOLS
Motto: Forward!
Animal: Badger
Wild Life Animal: White tailed deer
Domestic Animal: Dairy Cow
Bird: Robin
Fish: Musky (muskellunge)
Insect: Honeybee
Flower: Wood violet
Tree: Sugar maple
Mineral: Galena
Rock: Red granite
Song: "On Wisconsin"
GEO-FACS
Area: 56,153 sq. mi.
Rank in Area: 26th
Length (n/s): 320 mi.
Width (e/w): 295 mi.
Highest Point: 1,952 ft. (Timms Hill)
Lowest Point: 581 ft. (Lake Michigan)
Mean Elevation: 1,050 ft.
Temperature, Extreme Range: 168 degrees
Number of Counties: 72
POPULATION
Total: 4,751,000 (1983)
Rank: 16th
Density: 87 persons per sq. mi.
Principal Cities: Milwaukee, 636,236; Madison, 170,616; Green Bay, 87,899; Racine, 85,725; Kenosha, 77,685; West Allis, 63,982; Appleton, 58,913
EDUCATION
Schools: 2,898 elementary and secondary
Higher: 65
VITAL STATISTICS
Births (1980/83): 242,000
Deaths (1980/83): 133,000
Hospitals: 163
Drinking Age: 19
INTERESTING PEOPLE
Robert Marion La Follette, Robert M. La Follette, Jr., Frank Lloyd Wright, Christopher Latham Sholes, Allen Lapham, Ole Evinrude, Edna Ferber, Harry Houdini, Orson Welles, Stephen M. Babcock, Vinnie Ream, Hamlin Garland, Ben Hecht, Carrie Jacobs Bond, Tomah (Chief of the Menominees)
WHEN DID IT HAPPEN?
1634: First exploration, Jean Nicolet
1673: Marquette and Jolliet travel Wisconsin, discover upper Mississippi
1763: English claim recognized
1783: Treaty of Paris includes Wisconsin in U.S.
1832: Black Hawk goes to war
1848: Statehood
1854: Founding of Republican Party at Ripon
1871: Forest fire disaster
1901: La Follette is Governor
1917: State capitol finished
1948: Centennial year
1957: Braves win World Series
1983: Largest population gain in Midwest

INDEX to this volume

"Able McLaughlins, The" (book), 49
Accault, Michel, 73
Adams, Cuyler, 79
Addams, Jane, 21
Adena estate (OH), 99
Adena people, 28, 99
Agnew, Spiro, 62
Agriculture, 22, 37, 47, 48, 49, 50, 51, 64, 79, 92, 108, 120, 121
Airlines, passenger, 65, 92, 93
Airplanes, 62, 66, 106
Airports, 23
Akron, OH, 107
Alexandria, MN, 75
Algoma, WI, 121
Algonquin Indians, 71, 114
Allcorn, John, 38
Allouez, Claude, 115
Alpena, MI, 65
Altar Room (IN World War Mem.), 39
Alton, IL, 15
Aluminum, 106, 122
Amana, IA, 45, 51, 52, 53
Amana Co., 51, 53
Amana colonies, 52
"American Gothic" (painting), 49
American Legion, 39
American Royal Livestock and Horse Show, 94
American settlements, 31
Anderson, Eugenie, 77
Anderson, IN, 37
Anheuser, Eberhard, 91
Anheuser-Busch Co., 91, 92
Ann Arbor, MI, 67
Apache wars, 90
Apostle islands (WI), 111, 124
Appalachian Mts., 30
Apple trees, 39, 51, 107
Appleby, John, 119
Apples, 51, 107
Appleseed, Johnny (Jonathan Chapman), 36*, 39, 107
Appleton, WI, 117, 121
Aquariums, 23, 67
Archaic people, 85, 99
Architects and architecture, 20, 24, 38, 80, 109, 119, 120, 123
Armstrong, Neil, 105
Art Center (Des Moines, IA), 53
Art Center (Milwaukee, WI), 122
Art Institute of Chicago, 24
Artists, 24, 36, 38, 49, 91, 92, 120
Assassinations, 19, 60, 106
Astronauts, 105
Astronomy, 49
Athens, OH, 15
Atomic Age, 20
Atomic bomb, 90
Authors, 21, 35, 49, 61, 62, 78, 89, 91, 104, 107
Automobile industry, 65
Automobiles, 37, 63, 92, 107, 117
Aviation, 65, 77, 93, 104, 106
Aztalan, WI, 113, 114
Aztec people, 99, 113
B-24 Bombers, 62
Babcock, Stephen M., 119
Babe (Bunyan's blue ox), 81
Badgers (animal), 115, 120
Baha'i Temple (Wilmette, IL), 24
Balance Rock (WI), 111*
Bald eagles, 94
Baltimore, MD, 55
Baraboo, WI, 113, 123
Barberton, OH, 108
Barges, 93
Barite, 92
Baseball, 24, 80, 91, 93, 94, 104, 109, 118
Basketball, 24
Bass Islands (OH), 99
Battle Creek, MI, 64
Battle of Bad Axe, 115
Battle of Chattanooga, 61
Battle of Fallen Timbers, 102
Battle of Fort Meigs, 102
Battle of Fort Stephanson, 102
Battle of Gettysburg, 61*, 75
Battle of Iuka, 46
Battle of Lake Erie, 60, 102, 103*
Battle of Little Big Horn, 62
Battle of Raisin River, 102
Battle of Shiloh, 117
Battle of Westport, 88
Battle of Wilson's Creek, 46
Bean Blossom, IN, 38
Beaumont, William, 63, 119
Beaver Island (MI), 57, 60, 66
Bedford, IN, 37

Beer, 121
Belleville, IL, 22
Beloit, WI, 121
Bemidji, MN, 81
"Ben Hur" (book), 36
Benton, Thomas Hart (artist), 87, 91
Benton, Thomas Hart (senator), 90
Benton Harbor, MI, 28
Bertoia, Harry, 24
Bettendorf, IA, 51
Beveridge, Albert J., 35
Bienville, Celeron de, 100, 101
"Big Mac" (bridge), 12*, 62
Big Sioux River, 41, 53
Big Springs, MO, 83
"Big Three" (automobiles), 65
Bird Effigy Mound (IA), 43*
Black Hawk (chief), 7*, 17, 115
Black Hawk War, 17, 21, 115
Black River (MO), 83
Black River (WI), 113
Black Robes (priests), 115
Bloomer, Amelia, 50
Bloomers, 50
Blooming Grove, OH, 106
Bloomington, IN, 36, 37, 38
Bloomington, MN, 80
Blue ox, Babe, 81
Blues (music), 91
Boatload of Knowledge, 32
Bois de Sioux River, 69
Bond, Carrie Jacobs, 120
Bond, Shadrach, 17
Boone, Daniel, 71
Boone, IA, 50
Booth, Sherman M., 116
Border War, Michigan-Ohio, 103
Border disputes, 44, 60, 89, 97, 103
Botanical Center (Des Moines, IA), 53
Botanical Garden (St. Louis, MO), 93
Bottineau, Pierre, 81
Boundaries, 13, 28, 31, 41, 44, 55, 57, 60, 65, 69, 74, 83, 97, 99, 103, 113
Boundary disputes, 44, 60, 89, 97, 103
Bouquet, Henry, 101
Bourbeuse River, 85
Bowling Hall of Fame and Museum, 94
Bradley, Omar M., 89
Brainard, MN, 81
Breakfast food, 64
Breckenridge, MN, 69
Breckenridge, MO, 91
Brookfield Zoo, 23
Brooks, Gwendolyn, 21
Brown County, IN, 38
Browns Valley, MN, 71
Browns Valley Man, 71
Brule, Etienne, 57
Brule River, 111
Brush, Charles F., 107
Bryon, William Jennings, 89
Buchanan, James, 116
Buckeye (nickname), 103
Buckingham Fountain, 24
Buffalo, NY, 106
Buffalo Bill (William F. Cody), 50
Buffaloes (bison), 22, 50, 71, 72, 92, 101
Bull Shoals Lake, 83
Bunche, Ralph J., 63
Bunyan, Paul, 81, 113
Burger, Warren, 77
Burlington, IA, 44, 52
Burns Harbor, IN, 34
Burnside, Ambrose, 34
Busch, Adolphus, 91
Busch Gardens, 91
Bush Stadium, 91, 93
Butterfat, 119
Cadillac, Antoine de la Mothe, 58, 67
Cahokia, IL, 15, 16
Cahokia Mounds Park, 25
Calder, Alexander, 24
Calico RR, 45
Candy, 23
Cannibals, 114
Canton, OH, 108
Canyon of the St. Croix River, 81
Capital Centre (St. Paul, MN), 80
Capitals, state, 13, 29*, 32, 39, 42*, 45, 53, 60, 67, 74, 80, 94, 103, 112*, 116, 122
Capitol, U.S., 95, 120
Capitol domes, 67, 80, 122
Capitols, state, 13, 17, 25, 26*, 33, 39, 40*, 53, 54*, 67, 68*, 76, 80, 82*, 94, 95*, 109, 116, 122*
Carmichael, Hoagland (Hoagy), 36
Carnegie, Dale, 91
Carson, Johnny, 50

Caruthersville, MO, 85
Carver, George Washington, 49, 92
Cash register, 104, 106
Cass, Lewis, 60
Catfish Creek, IA, 44
Cathedral of St. Paul (St. Paul, MN), 80
Catholic Sisters of St. Francis, 77
Catlin, George, 72
Catt, Carrie Chapman, 50
Cavelier, Rene Robert (Sieur de La Salle), 16, 28, 58, 86, 100
Caves, 83, 85, 94
Cedar Falls, IA, 53
Cedar Rapids, IA, 51, 53
Cedar River, 41
Celeron claim plates, 100, 101
Cellophane, 51
Cement, 64
Cenotaphs, 39
Center of Science & Industry (Des Moines, IA), 53
Century of Progress, 20
Ceramics, 36
Chagall, Marc, 24
Champlain, Samuel de, 28
Chapman, Jonathan (Johnny Appleseed), 36*, 39, 107
Charcoal, 93
Charles City, IA, 50, 51
Charleston, IL, 24
Chequamegon Bay (WI), 111
Cherokee Indians, 87
Cherries, 64
Cherry Festival, 66
Chicago, IL, 3*, 13, 14*, 17, 18, 20, 23, 24, 61, 90, 93, 117
"Chicago Picasso" (sculpture), 24*
Chicago River, 16
Chicago Symphony Orchestra, 24
Child labor laws, 117
Children's Museum (IN), 39
Children's Theater (MN), 80
Chimney (MN), 71
Chippewa Indians (Ojibwa), 28, 43, 57, 71, 72, 74, 76
Chippewa River, 70, 71, 113
Chisholm, A. M., 77
Cholera, 63
Chouteau, Auguste Pierre, 86
Christmas trees, 79
Chronology, 26, 40, 54, 68, 82, 96, 110, 124
Chrysler, Walter P., 65
Church of Jesus Christ of Latter Day Saints, 18, 88, 103
Churchill, Winston, 89, 90
Churchill, Winston (novelist), 91
Cincinnati, OH, 98*, 102, 103, 104, 106, 108, 109
Cincinnati Art Museum, 109
Cincinnati Bengals (football), 109
Cincinnati Reds (baseball), 104, 109
Cincinnati Symphony, 109
Cincinnati Zoo, 109
Circus World Museum, 123
Circus festival, 39
Circuses, 39, 113, 123
City Center Square (Kansas City, KS), 94
Civic Arts & Science Center (St. Paul, MN), 80
Civil War, 19, 33, 35, 45, 46, 61, 62, 67, 75, 77, 88, 89, 106, 117
Clark, George Rogers, 16, 25, 30, 31
Clark, James Beauchamp (champ), 90
Clark, William, 44, 87
Clarksville, IN, 31
Cleaveland, Moses, 109
Clemens, Samuel L. (Mark Twain), 89, 91, 119
Cleveland, OH, 102, 104, 107, 109*
Cleveland Health Museum, 109
Cleveland Symphony Orchestra, 109
Clinton, IA, 51, 52
Clowes Hall (Indianapolis, IN), 39
Coal, 22, 36, 37, 50, 64, 78, 92, 93, 108
Cody, William F. (Buffalo Bill), 50
Columbia, MO, 94
Columbus, IN, 35
Columbus, OH, 103, 109
Communal settlements, 52, 103
Communications, 23, 45
Compac-Facs, 26, 40, 53, 54, 67, 68, 81, 82, 95, 109, 110, 124
Composers, 36, 49, 91, 107, 120
Computers, 49
Conservancy Act of 1914, 104
Conservation, 50, 64, 75, 76, 94, 120
Constitutions, 60
Contour farming, 121
Convention Under the Oaks, 60

Conventions, 18, 60, 76, 89
Conventions, political, 18, 76, 89
Coolidge, Calvin, 47, 49
Copper, 60, 64, 92
Copper Culture people, 113
Corn, 22, 37, 49, 50, 108
Cornstalk (chief), 101
Corydon, IN, 33
Coronado, Francisco Vasquez de, 85
Coshocton, OH, 101
Country Club Plaza (Kansas City, MO), 94*
County War Mem. (Milwaukee, WI), 122
Coureurs de bois (trappers), 58
Covered Bridge Festival, 38
Covered wagons, 93
Cranberries, 121
Creole Ball (Vincennes, IN), 38
Croghan, George, 100
Crown Center (Kansas City, MO), 91, 94
Crystal Court Square (Minneapolis, MN), 80
Cultural Gardens (Cleveland, OH), 109
Currier and Ives, 8
Custer, George Armstrong, 62
Customs, Indian, 16, 28, 44, 57, 72, 85, 100, 114
Customs, prehistoric, 28, 99, 113, 114
Cuyahoga River, 97
Cuyuna Range, 79
Cypripedium reginae (orchid), 78
D-Day, 62
Dacatur, IL, 24
Dacotah Indians, 6*, 71
Dairy products, 19, 22, 120, 123
Daley, Richard J., 20
Daley Plaza (Chicago, IL), 24*
Danish settlements, 76
Darling, J. N. "Ding", 49
Daughters of the American Revolution, 33
Davenport, IA, 52
Davis, Jefferson, 61
Day, John Other, 75
Dayton, George Nelson, 77
Dayton, OH, 106, 107
Dayton Central High School (OH), 107
De Soto, Hernando, 85, 86
Dearborn, MI, 66
Dearborn Inn (MI), 66
Decatur, IL, 24
Deer, 22, 50, 101
Deere and Co., 22, 51
Defoe Co., 62
Delaware Indians, 32, 87, 100
Deming, W. Edwards, 49
Depression of 1893, 46
Depression of 1929, 47, 61, 76, 104
Des Moines, IA, 42*, 45, 51, 52*, 53
Des Moines River, 41, 44
Des Plaines River, 16
Detroit, MI, 31, 55, 56*, 58, 59*, 60, 62, 63, 64, 65, 66, 67, 92
Detroit Civic Center, 66
Detroit River, 55, 65, 67
Dewey, Thomas E., 62
Diamond, MO, 82
Diamond (elephant), 39
Dillon, Lyman, 45
Disasters, natural, 13, 20, 25, 34, 46, 47, 59, 61, 75, 76, 87, 89, 104, 117
Disney, Walt, 91
"Dixie" (song), 38
Domes, capitol, 67, 80, 122
Doolittle, James H., 89
Door County, WI, 111, 123
Douglas, Stephen A., 19, 21
Douglas, William O., 77
Dousman, Hercules, 124
Dred Scott decision, 88
Droughts, 47, 76
Du Gay (Catholic priest), 73
Du Lhut, Sieur (Daniel Greysolon), 73
Dubuque, IA, 45, 51, 52
Dubuque, Julien, 44
Duluth, MN, 75, 81
Duluth (Sieur du Lhut), 73
Dunbar, Paul Laurence, 107*
Dunmore, Lord, 101
Dust storms, 47, 76
Dutch settlements, 45*, 67
Dvorak, Antonin, 49
Eagle Point Park (Dubuque, IA), 51
Eagle River, 122
Eagles, 117
Early Man, 85
Earthquakes, 18
East Cleveland, OH, 107
East St. Louis, IL, 23
Economy, 9, 23, 37, 51, 65, 79, 93, 108, 121

125

Edison, Thomas A., 66, 106, 107
Effigy Mounds Nat. Mon., 43, 52
Egg Harbor, WI, 123
Eisenhower, Mamie, 50
Electrical industry, 20, 122
Electricity, 33, 117
Electronics industry, 79
Elephants, 83
Elizabeth II of England, 118
Elkhart, IN, 37
Elliot Hall of Music (Purdue Univ.), 39
Elwood, IN, 35
Ely, MN, 81
Emmett, Daniel, 107
English vs. French wars, 30, 58, 73, 101
Entertainers, 36, 49, 50, 91
Erie, PA, 100
Erie Canal, 18, 32, 60, 103
Erie Indians, 100
Estherville, IA, 46
European settlements, 86, 115
Evansville, IN, 33
Evinrude, Ole, 119
Executions, 75
Explorers, 16, 28, 30, 43, 44, 57, 58, 69, 72, 73, 74, 85, 86, 91, 97, 99, 100, 114, 115
Fantastic Caverns (MO) 94
Far West, MO, 88
Farmer-Labor Party, 76
Ferber, Edna, 120
Ferris, George, 20
Festivals, 38, 39, 45*, 66, 80, 81, 94, 123
"Fiddle back" mound, 28
Field, Eugene, 91
Field, Marshall, 21
Finnish settlements, 76
Fir trees, 75
Firehoses, 107
Fires, 20, 59, 61, 75, 76, 88, 117
First Regiment (IA), 46
First Regiment (MN), 75
First State Capitol (MO), 94
Fishing, sport, 22, 78
Fitzgerald, F. Scott, 78
Flags, 33, 39, 44, 67, 74
Flambeau River, 113
"Flamingo" (sculpture), 24
Flood control, 75, 104
Floods, 13, 25, 34, 104
Flour processing, 119
Floyd, Charles, 44, 53
Fluorspar, 22
Ford, Edsel, 64
Ford, Gerald R., 62, 67
Ford, Henry, 63*, 64, 65, 66
Ford Foundation, 64
Ford Motor Co., 62, 63
Ford Museum, 66*
Ford Peace Ship, 63
Ford's River Rouge plant, 67
Forest Products Lab., U.S., 121
Forest industry, 64, 70, 121
Forests, 22, 64, 76, 78, 81, 92, 99, 117, 120
Fort Ancient State Mem. (OH), 99
Fort Ancient people, 28
Fort Beauharnois, 73
Fort Dearborn, 17
Fort Dearborn Massacre, 17
Fort Defiance, 102
Fort Mackinac, 66
Fort Madison, IA, 44, 51
Fort McKay, 115
Fort Meigs, 102
Fort Miami, 30, 31
Fort Michilimackinac, 12*, 58, 66
Fort Necessity, 101
Fort Osage, MO, 87
Fort Ouiatenon, 30
Fort Recovery, 102
Fort Ridgely, 75
Fort Snelling, 74, 76
Fort Snelling State Park (MN), 76, 80
Fort St. Charles, 73
Fort Stephanson, 102
Fort Wayne, IN, 28, 31, 37, 39
Fort de Charters, 16, 25
Fort of the Miamis, 30, 31
Fortune 500 companies, 51
Fossils, 83, 85
Fox Indians, 16, 17
Fox River, 113, 115
Franklin, Benjamin, 74
Freedom of religion, 88, 94, 103
Fremont, OH, 105, 108
French Canada, 58, 73
French settlements, 16, 30, 57, 86
French vs. English wars, 30, 58, 73, 101
Fringed gentian, 78
Fritchie, Barbara, 66
Fulton, MO, 89, 90
Fur trade, 16, 30, 57, 74, 77, 86, 92, 100, 115, 124
Furniture industry, 64, 67

Gabriel's Rock (IN), 38
Galena, IL, 17, 18, 20*, 21
Galtier, Lucian, 74
Garland, Hamlin, 120
Gary, IN, 37
Gas and oil, 22, 23, 36, 64, 92, 108
Gas station pumps, 37
Gasoline engine cars, 65
Gateway Arch (Jefferson Nat. Expansion Mem.), 86*, 89, 93
Gaultier, Pierre (Sieur de La Verendrye), 73
General Electric Co., 107
General Motors Co., 65
Geography, 13, 15, 22, 27, 28, 31, 41, 55, 57, 69, 71, 93, 97, 99, 111, 113
Geology, 13, 22, 27, 36, 41, 57, 71, 83, 99, 111, 113
Gerald Ford Library, 67
Gerald Ford Museum, 67
German settlements, 122
Gettysburg of the West (Battle of Westport), 88
Gilbert, Cass, 80
"Girl of the Limberlost, A" (book), 35
Gist, Christopher, 100, 101
Glaciers, 13, 22, 27, 41, 57, 71, 99, 113
Glass, 22, 37, 107
Glencoe, MN, 75
Glenn, John, 105
Glover, Joshua, 116
Gnaw Bone, IN, 38
Goodrich, Benjamin Franklin, 107
Graham Cave (MO), 85
Grand Portage, MN, 74
Grand Portage Nat. Mon., 74
Grand Rapids, MI, 64, 65, 67
Grand River, 97
Grant, Ulysses S., 10, 19, 20, 21, 36, 105, 108
Great Lakes, 13, 17, 18, 22, 28, 55, 58, 65, 69, 97, 102, 105, 113, 118
Great Miami River, 97
"Greatest Show on Earth, The" (circus), 123
Green Bay, WI, 73, 111, 113, 114, 115, 120, 123
Green Bay Packers (football), 123
Greenfield, IN, 35
Greenfield Village, MI, 66
Gresham, Bethel, 33
Gresham, James B., 39
Grey, Zane, 107
Greybeards, 46
Greysolon, Daniel (Sieur du Lhut), 73
Grierson, Benjamin H., 19
"Griffon" (ship), 58
Grindstone City, MI, 65
Grinnell, IA, 46
Groseilliers, Sieur de, 115
Guerilla warfare, 88, 89
Guggenheim Museum of Art (NYC), 120
Gulf of Mexico, 28, 30, 83, 99
Guthrie, Tyrone, 80
Gypsum, 50

H. Roe Bartle Exposition Hall (Kansas City, MO), 94
Hadley, Paul, 33
Hagenbeck-Wallace circus, 39
"Hair Buyer" Hamilton, Henry, 30, 31, 58, 101
Hall, Charles Martin, 106
Hall, James Norman, 49
Hall, Joyce C., 91
Hamilton, Henry (Hair Buyer), 30, 31, 58, 101
Hancock Center., Chicago, 11*
Handy, W. C., 91
Hannibal, MO, 89
Harbors, 81, 111
Hargems, Charles, 88
Harmony, MN, 75
Harness racing, 46
Harrison, Benjamin, 106
Harrison, William Henry, 31, 32, 33, 35, 106, 108
Harry S. Truman Sports Complex (Kansas City, MO), 94
Hart, Charles W., 51
Harvey, Cordelia, 117
Harvey, Louis P., 117
Hay, Merle, 46
Hayes, Rutherford B., 105, 108
Hayes Mem., 105
Hecht, Ben, 21
Hemingway, Ernest, 21
Hennepin, Louis, 73
Henry, Patrick, 16, 30
Hetuck (buckeye), 103
Hiatt, Jesse, 46
Hickory, WI, 123
Highways, 23, 24, 46, 93, 103

Hill, James J., 77
Hinckley, MN, 75
Hoard, William, 119
Hoaxes, 73
Hockey, 24
Hocking Hills State Park (OH), 97*
Hocking River, 97
Holland, MI, 61, 67
Honey War, 44, 89
Hoover Library, 47, 52
Hoover, Herbert, 47, 48
Hopewell people, 28, 99, 100*
Horlick, William, 120
Horse racing, 46
"Hot dog" (origin), 105
Hough, Emerson, 49
Houghton, Douglass, 60
Houghton, MI, 55
"House that Jack (a mule) built" (Bellaire, OH), 109
Hubbard, Frank McKinney (Kim), 36
Hudson, Joseph L., 64
Hudson Bay, 69
Humphrey, Hubert H., 76
Hunting, 78
Huron Indians, 57, 100
Hurst, Fanny, 91
Hutchinson, MN, 75
Ice-cream cones, 89
Illini Indians, 16, 28, 43, 44
Illinois (main article), 13
Illinois River, 13, 16
Independence, IA, 46
Independence, MO, 90, 94
Independence Hall (replica), 66*
"Indian Lament" (music), 49
Indian Peace Mem. Statue, 80
Indian customs, 16, 28, 44, 57, 72, 85, 100, 114, 124
Indian leaders, 17, 35, 58, 75, 101, 114
Indian pipes (plant), 78
Indian rights, 76
Indian wars, 17, 31, 32, 58, 74, 75, 85, 86, 87, 102, 106
Indiana (main article), 27
Indiana Dunes, 27, 34
Indiana Dunes Nat. Lakeshore, 34
Indiana Univ., 38, 39
Indiana World War Mem., 39
Indianapolis, IN, 29*, 32, 33, 35, 37, 38, 39
Indianapolis 500 race, 39*
Indianapolis Symphony, 39
Indians, 15, 16, 17, 25, 28, 30, 31, 32, 43, 57, 58, 59, 60, 62, 71, 72*, 74, 75, 77, 80, 85, 86, 87*, 89, 99, 101, 102, 114, 115
Indians, displacement, 16, 28, 43, 57, 71, 87, 100, 115
Industrialists, 21, 64, 77, 107
Industry, 34, 37, 51, 65, 79, 107, 117, 119, 121, 123
Institute of Paper Chemistry, 121
Insurance, 51
International Harvester (Navistar), 22
Interstate Park (MN/WI), 124
Inventors and inventions, 21, 104, 106, 117, 119, 120
Iowa (main article), 41
Iowa City, IA, 45, 53
Iowa State Univ., 46, 48, 49
Ioway Indians, 43, 85
Iron County, MO, 85
Iron Curtain speech, 89, 90
Iron ore, 76, 78, 92, 120
Iron processing, 64, 76
Iroquois Indians, 57, 100
Irving, John, 49
Isle Royale, NY, 57, 64
Isle Royale Nat. Park, 66
Itasca Lake, 69
Itasca State Park (MN), 81
Ivory Soap, 108
J. I. Case Co., 22
Jackson, MI, 64
James, Jesse, 89
Jefferson City, MO, 94
Jefferson Nat. Expansion Mem., 86*, 89, 93
Jesuits, 86
John Deere Co., 22
John Herron Art Institute (IN), 39
John Paul II, Pope, 47
Johnny Appleseed Mem. Park (Fort Wayne, IN), 30
Johnson, John, 22
Jolliet, Louis, 15, 16, 43, 44, 86, 115
Joplin, MO, 94
Kansas City, MO, 85, 87, 89, 91, 92, 93, 94
Kansas City Chiefs (football), 94
Kantor, MacKinlay, 49
Kaskaskia, IL, 13, 16, 17, 30
Kaskaskia Bell State Park (IL), 25
Kelleys Island (OH), 99

Kelleys Island State Park (OH), 99
Kellogg, Frank B, 77
Kellogg, W. K., 64
Kellogg-Briand Peace Pact, 77
Kelly, Pat, 120
Kensington, MN, 73
Kensington Runestone (reproduction), 73*
Kettering, Charles, 104, 106
Kickapoo Indains, 87
Kimmswick, MO, 83
Kindergarten, 116
King, Charles Bird, 7, 30
King, Charles G., 65
Kirkwood, Samuel J., 45
Kock, Albrecht, 85
Kohler of Kohler, WI, 122
Kokomo, IN, 28
Korean War, 62
Kresge, Sebastian S., 64
Ku Klux Klan, 34
La Crosse, WI, 124
La Follette, Philip Fox, 119
La Follette, Robert M. Jr., 119
La Follette, Robert M. Sr., 117, 118*
La Salle, Sieur de (Robert Cavelier), 16, 28, 58, 86, 100
Labor movement, 61
Laclede, MO, 90
Laclede's Landing, MO, 93
Lady of the Lake, 71
Lady's slipper (cypripedium reginae), 78
Lafayette, IN, 39
Lake Agassiz (prehistoric), 71
Lake Aitkin, 71
Lake Chicago (prehistoric), 13
Lake Country (MO), 96*
Lake Duluth, 71
Lake Erie, 58, 60, 97, 100, 102, 103
Lake Geneva, WI, 122
Lake Huron, 58
Lake Mendota, 123
Lake Michigan, 13, 17, 18, 22, 23, 27, 34, 65, 111, 113, 122
Lake Michigan dunes, 36
Lake Pepin, 71, 73, 75
Lake Superior, 69, 71, 73, 76, 78, 81, 111, 120
Lake Taneycomo, 83
Lake Winnebago, 113
Lake Winnipeg, 73
Lake of the Ozarks, 83
Lake of the Woods, 69, 71
Lakes, 13, 28, 41, 55, 69, 71, 83, 94, 96*, 97, 113, 124
Lamar, MO, 89
Lancaster, OH, 106
Land grants, 44
Lanfield (Mentor, OH), 109
Lansing, MI, 60, 65, 67
Laona, WI, 121
Lapham, Increase, 119
Lawnfield (Mentor, OH), 109
Le Claire, Ia, 52
Le Mars, IA, 46
Le Sueur, MN, 77
Lead mining, 44
Leavenworth, Henry H., 74
Lee, Albert, 44
Leech Lake, 74
Legends, 28, 81
Lewis, Henry, 6
Lewis, Meriwether, 44, 87
Lewis, Sinclair, 78
Lewis and Clark expedition, 44, 53, 87
Liberty Bell of the West, 25
Liguest, Pierre Laclede, 86
Limestone quarries, 65
Lincoln, Abraham, 13, 18*, 19, 21, 24, 25, 33, 34, 35, 46, 75, 120
Lincoln, IL, 19
Lincoln, Robert Todd, 25
Lincoln Boyhood Nat. Mem., 33*
Lincoln Nat. Mem. Highway, 24
Lincoln Park Zoo (Chicago, IL), 23
Lincoln's funeral procession, 19*
Lincoln's tomb, 25*
Lincoln-Douglas debate, 21
Lindbergh, Charles A., 77
Litchfield, MN, 75
Little Crow (chief), 75
Little Miami River, 97
Little Norway, WI, 123
Little Pigeon Creek, 34
Little Turtle (chief Meshekinnoquah), 31, 35
Little Wabash River, 30
Livestock industry, 22, 51, 79, 92
Living History Farms Museum, 47, 53
Logan (chief), 101
Logans elm, 101
Longfellow, Henry Wadsworth, 72
Lord Dunmore's War, 101
Lost River, 28
Louisiana Purchase, 44, 45, 74, 87

126

Louisiana Purchase Expo., 89
Louisiana Territory, 44, 86, 87
Lucas, Robert, 44
Lumber and wood products, 64, 79, 93, 121
Lumbering, 121
Mackinac Bridge, 12*, 62
Mackinac Island, MI, 57, 66
Madison, WI, 112*, 116, 117, 120, 121, 122, 123
Magna Charta of the Northwest, 102
"Maine" (Battleship), 46
Malted milk, 120
Manganese, 78
Manistee, MI, 61
Manitou Island (MI), 57
Manufacturing, 23, 37, 52, 61, 64, 67, 79, 92, 107, 108, 121
Maple syrup, 72
Marietta, OH, 102
Marion, OH, 108
"Mark Twain" (river call), 91
Marquette, Jacques, 15, 16, 43, 44, 57, 86, 115
Marshalltown, IA, 51
Mascouten Indians, 16
Mason, Stevens T., 60
Mason City, IA, 49
Massacres, 17, 59, 62, 101, 102, 115
Mastodons, 83, 85
Mattoon, IL, 22, 23
Maumee River, 30, 97
Mayo, Charles, 77
Mayo, William J., 77
Mayo, William Worrell, 77
Mayo Clinic, 77
Mayo Family, 77, 81
Maytag Co., 51
McArthur, Duncan, 60
McCormick, Cyrus H., 21
McCutcheon, John T., 36
McDonnell Aircraft Co., 92
McGregor, IA, 43
McGregor Heights, IA, 52
McGuffey, William Holmes, 107
McGuffey Readers, 107
McKinley, William, 48, 104*, 106, 109
McKinley Birthplace Nat. Mem., 109
Menard, Rene, 115
Menasha, WI, 121
Menlo Park, NJ, 66
Menominee Indians, 57, 114, 118, 122
Menominee River, 111
Menton, OH, 109
Meredith Pub. Co., 51
Merrit, Leonidas, 78
Merritt, Darwin R., 46
Mesabi Range, 78, 81
Meshekinnoquah (Little Turtle), 35
Mesquakie Indians, 43
Meteors, 81
Metropolitan Stadium (MN), 80
Miami Indians, 28, 31, 43, 57, 100, 101
Mica, 50, 78
Michener, James, 49
Michigamea Indians, 87
Michigan (main article), 55
Michigan National Guard, 62
Michigan State Police Headquarters, 66
Michigan's 24th regiment, 61*
Mies van der Rohe, Ludwig, 24
Milan, OH, 106
Milles, Carl, 80
Milwaukee, WI, 114, 116*, 121, 122
Milwaukee Braves (baseball), 118
Milwaukee Public Museum, 114
Milwaukee Summerfest, 122
Mineral Point, WI, 115, 123
Minerals and mining, 18, 22, 36, 37, 50, 64, 78, 79, 92, 93, 108, 115, 120, 121
Mink growing, 121
Minneapolis, MN, 70*, 73, 74, 76, 79, 80*
Minneapolis-Honeywell, 79
Minnehaha Falls, 80
Minnesota (main article), 69
Minnesota Man, 71
Minnesota Minning & Manufacturing (3M), 79
Minnesota Symphony Orchestra, 80
Minnesota Twins (baseball), 80
Mints, 64
Mishawaka, IN, 28
Mission of St. Francis Xavier, 115
Mississippi Delta, 82
Mississippi Embayment, 83
Mississippi River, 8, 13, 15, 16, 21, 30, 41, 45, 51, 52, 55, 69, 70, 71*, 74, 75, 79, 81, 83, 86, 88, 89, 91, 93, 94, 111, 113, 115, 123, 124
Mississippi Valley, 44, 85
Missouri (main article), 83
Missouri Compromise, 87
Missouri Indians, 43, 85
Missouri Ozarks, 83

Missouri River, 41, 44, 53, 83, 86, 87, 93
Mitchell Park Horticultural Conservatory (Milwaukee, WI), 122
Model T Ford, 65
Mondale, Walter, 76
Monks Mound (IL), 15
Monroe, James, 87
Monroe, WI, 123
Monsanto Chemical Co., 92
Montgomery County, MO, 85
Montgomery Ward Co., 64
Montour, Andrew, 100
Monument Circle (Indianapolis, IN), 39
Monuments, 25, 31, 39, 43, 52, 53, 80, 81, 89, 108
Mooresville, IN, 33
Moorhead, MN, 81
Moose, 64
Morgan, John Hunt, 33
Mormon religion, 18, 88, 103
Mormon settlements, 18, 60, 88
Mormons, 88, 94
Mormons displacement, 88, 94, 103
Morton, Oliver P., 33, 35
Morton Arboretum (IL), 24
Mound Builders, 15, 113
Mounds, prehistoric, 15, 28, 43, 57, 71, 85, 99, 109, 113
Mountains, 71
Mountains, prehistoric, 71
Muncie, IN, 37
Municipal Pier (Milwaukee, WI), 122
Museum of Amana History, 52
Museum of Natural History (Cincinnati, OH), 109
Museum of Science and Industry, 23
Museum of Westward Expansion, 93
Museums, 23, 24, 39, 52, 53, 66, 67, 80, 93, 100, 101, 109, 115, 122, 123
"Music Man, The" (musical play), 49
Muskingum River, 97
Names, origin, 34, 51, 58, 67, 79, 91, 103, 107, 122, 123
Nashville, IN, 36, 38
National Bowling Hall of Fame, 94
National Geographic Soc., 41
National Road, 103
Natural Bridges, 83
Nauvoo, IL, 18
Neenah, WI, 121
Neville Museum (Green Bay, WI), 115
New Glarus, WI, 123
New Harmony, IN, 32*, 38
New Madrid, MO, 87
New Orleans, LA, 21
New Salem, IL, 24
New Ulm, MN, 75
New York, NY, 91, 120
Niagara Cave, 81
Nichols, J. C., 94
Nichols Fountain (Kansas City, KS), 94*
Nicolet, Jean, 114, 115
Niles, MI, 64
Niles, OH, 105, 106
Nixon, Richard M., 62, 77
Nobel Prize, 21, 63, 77, 78
Normandy, France, 62
North Bend, OH, 106, 108
Northwest Co., 74
Northwest Ordinance, 31, 102
Northwest Territory, 31, 59, 74, 115
Norway pine, 78
Norwegian settlements, 76
Notre Dame Univ., 38*
O'Conner, Flannery, 49
O'Hare Airport, 20
O'Leary's cow, 20
Oak Ridge Cemetery, IL, 24
Oakville, IA, 43
Oats, 50
Ocheyedan Mound (IA), 43
Oconomowoc, WI, 122
Oconto, WI, 113, 115
Ohio (main article), 97
Ohio Co. of Associates, 102
Ohio Co. of Virginia, 100
Ohio River, 13, 16, 17, 18, 27, 28, 30, 32, 37, 83, 97, 100, 101, 102, 104
Ohio River Valley, 0
Ohio Univ., 107
Ohman, Olaf, 73
Oil and gas, 22, 23, 36, 64, 92, 108
Oil industry, 34
Ojibwa Indians (Chippewa), 28, 43, 57, 71, 72, 74, 76
Okoboji Lake, 41
Old Abe (eagle), 117
Old Village (prehistoric MO town), 85
Olds, Ransom E., 65
Oldsmobiles, 65
Omaha, NE, 53
Omaha Indians, 43
Ontonagon, MI, 64

Orange, OH, 106
Orchids, 78, 92
Oregon Trail, 88
Oriental Institute (Chicago, IL), 24
Orr, Robert D., 34
Osage Indians, 43, 85, 87
Osage River, 83
Osceola County, IA, 43
Oshkosh, WI, 114, 117
Oshkosh (chief), 114
Ottawa Indians, 16, 28, 43, 57
Otter Tail River, 69
Outboard motors, 119
Owen, Robert, 32
Owosso, MI, 62
Ozark Airlines, 92
Ozark Mts., 13, 94
Pageant of the Sault, 57, 58
Palmer, Potter, 21
Pana, IL, 22
Panama Canal, 121
Papermaking, 121
Paris, IL, 23
Parke County, IN, 38
Parr, Charles, 51
Parrant, Pierre (Pig's Eye), 74
Passenger pigeons, 120
Paul Bunyan Carnival, 81
Peat, 64, 78
Peebles, OH, 109
Pelican Rapids, MN, 71
Pemmican (dried buffalo meat), 71
Penney, J. C., 91
Peoples, 10, 21, 34, 48, 62, 76, 90, 105, 119
Perry, Oliver Hazard, 102, 103
Pershing, John J., 89, 90
Peru, IA, 51
Peru, IN, 36, 39
Peshtigo, WI, 117
Peters, G. W., 104
Pheasants, 50
Philadelphia, PA, 119
Philip (prince) of England, 118
Piankeshaw Indians, 16, 87
Piasa Bird, 15*
"Picasso, Chicago" (sculpture), 24*
Picasso, Pablo, 24
Pickawillany (OH Indian village), 101
Pike, Zebulon, 44, 74
Pikes Peak (IA), 44
Pillsbury, John Sargent, 77
Piper Bldg. (Minneapolis, MN), 80*
Pipestone, 72, 78
Pipestone Nat. Mon., 80
Pirates, 86, 102
Pitcherplant, 36
Plains Indians, 43
Plants, 22, 36, 78, 92
Plates, Celeron exploration, 100, 101
Poe, Edgar Allan, 66
Point Pleasant, OH, 108
Ponca Indians, 43
Pontiac (chief), 30, 58, 101
Pony Express, 88*, 92, 93, 94
Popcorn, 50, 108
Pope, Nathaniel, 17
Popes, 47
Poplar Bluff, MO, 85
Poplar tree, 36, 38
Population, 23, 34, 59, 60, 75, 116, 118
Port Huron, MI, 55
Port of Chicago, 20, 23
Portage, WI, 113
Portage River, 97
Portaging, 113
Porter, Cole, 36
Porter, Gene Stratton, 35
Ports, 20, 23, 34, 65, 76, 105, 111, 118
Post, C. W., 64
Potawatomi Indians, 16, 17, 43, 57
Poultry products, 22
Pow-wows, 25
Powell, William H., 114
Poynette, WI, 120
Prairie du Chien, WI, 115, 123
Prehistoric customs, 28, 99, 113, 114
Prehistoric mounds, 15, 28, 43, 57, 71, 85, 99, 109, 113
Prehistoric mts., 71
Prehistoric peoples, 13, 25, 28, 43, 57, 71, 85, 99, 109, 113
Prehistoric settlements, 85
Prehistoric weapons, 57
Prehistoric wildlife, 83, 85
Presque Isle, MI, 65
"Prince of India, The" (book), 36
"Pro Patria" (statue), 39
Proclamation of 1763, 30
Proctor, Henry A., 32
Progressive Republican Party, 118
Prophet (Tenskwatawa), 30*, 32, 35

Prophetstown, IN, 32
Pulitzer, Joseph, 91
Pulitzer Prize, 21, 35, 49, 91
Pulman, George, 21
Pumpkin Center, MO, 91
Purdue Univ., 38
Purple fringed orchid, 92
Put-in-Bay, OH, 102
Quaker Oats Co., 51
Raccoon River, 97
Race relations, 62
Racine, WI, 116
Raddison, Pierre Esprit, 115
Raido, 23, 123
Railroads, 23, 32, 45, 46, 76, 77, 93
Raisin River Massacre, 59
Ramsey, Alexander, 74
Randall, Alexander, 117
Rashford, Coles, 116
Ray, Robert, 47
Reagan, Ronald, 105
Ream, Vinnie, 120
Reconstruction, 89
Recreation, 65, 66, 81
Red Banks (WI), 114
Red Lake, 69, 73
Red Lake River, 69
Red Oak, IA, 46
Red River Valley, 73, 79, 81
Red River of the North, 69, 79, 81
Red granite, 121
Religious co-op, 52
Religious freedom, 88, 94, 103
Renaissance Center (Detroit, MI), 62, 67
Reorganized Church of Jesus Christ of Latter Day Saints, 94
Republican Party, 60, 116
Research, 20
Resources, 22, 36, 50, 60, 64, 78, 79, 92, 101, 108
Restoration, 25, 93, 94, 108
Revolutionary War, 16, 30, 31, 58, 74, 86, 101, 113
Rhinelander, WI, 124
Rib Mt., 113, 120
Rice, David, 91
Richard, Gabriel, 59, 63
Richland Center, WI, 119
Riley, James Whitcomb, 35
Ringling Brothers, 123
Ritty, James, 104, 106
Riverbend Music Center, OH, 109
Riverfront Stadium (OH), 109
Rivers, 13, 16, 27, 28, 41, 55, 69, 71, 83, 93, 97, 111, 113
Roc River, 113
Rochester, MN, 77, 81
Rockefeller, John D. Sr., 104
Rockefeller Park (Cleveland, OH), 109
Rockwell, Norman, 63
Rocky Mts., 99
Rogers, Robert, 58
Rolvaag, Ole Edvart, 78
Roofless Church (IN), 32*, 38
Roosevelt, F. D., 35, 49, 89, 90
Roosevelt, Theodore, 48, 76, 106, 118
Root, Jim, 76
Rose Island (IN), 28
Royal English Rangers, 58
Rubber products, 107
Russell, Lillian, 50
Rutherford B. Hayes Lib. and Mus. State Mem. (OH), 108
Sabin, J. C., 46
Salmon, 22
Salt and salt mining, 22, 64, 108
San Francisco, CA, 106
Sandburg, Carl, 21
Sandusky, OH, 99
Sandusky River, 97
Santa Fe Trail, 88
Sargent, Winthrop, 31
Sauk Centre, MN, 75, 78
Sauk Indians, 16, 17
Sault Sainte Marie, MI, 57, 66
Scandinavian settlements, 76
Schoolcraft, Henry R., 69
Schurz, (Mrs.) Carl, 116
Scioto River, 97
Scott, Dred, 88
Sears Tower (Chicago, IL), 20
"Seawing" (steamer), 75
Selfridge, Harry Gordon, 64
Serpent Mound State Mem. (OH), 109
Settlements, American, 31
Settlements, Danish, 76
Settlements, Dutch, 45*, 67
Settlements, European, 86, 115
Settlements, Finnish, 76
Settlements, French, 16, 30, 57, 86
Settlements, German, 122
Settlements, Mormon, 18, 60, 88
Settlements, Norwegian, 76

127

Settlements, Scandinavian, 76
Settlements, Swedish, 76
Settlements, Swiss, 123
Settlements, Welsh, 123
Settlements, prehistoric, 85
"Seventeen" (book), 85
Shanks, Charles B., 107
Shawnee Indians, 28, 35, 100, 101
Sheaffer Pen Co., 51
Sheboygan, WI, 122
Shedd Aquarium, 23
Sheridan, Philip H., 106
Sherman, William T., 106
Sholes, Christopher L., 117, 119
Sibley, Henry Hastings, 75, 77
Sideburns, 34
Silver, 92
Silver Dollar City, MO, 94
Sioux City, IA, 44, 53
Sioux Indians, 71, 72*, 74, 75, 77, 114
Sisseton Indians, 43
Skyscrapers, 20
Slavery, 18, 33, 60, 75, 87, 88, 89, 103, 116
Smith, Hiram, 120
Smith, Joseph, 18, 103
Smoke tree, 92
Snelling, Josiah, 74
Snowshoes, 57
Soccer, 24
Sod houses, 75
Soldiers and Sailors Mon. (IN), 39
Somerset, OH, 106
"Song of Hiawatha, The" (poem), 72
Soo Canal, 65
South Amherst, OH, 108
South Bend, IN, 28, 37, 38
Southern Ozarks, 13
Soybeans, 50, 92, 108
Spillville, IA, 49
Spirit Lake, 41
Split Rock Lighthouse (MN), 78*
Sports, 24, 38, 46, 80, 91, 93, 94, 104, 109, 118, 123, 124
Spring Green, WI, 120, 123
Springfield, IL, 24, 25
Springfield, MO, 94
Springs, natural, 83
Sprout, Ebenezer, 103
Squirral Cage Jail (Council Bluffs, IA), 53
St. Anthony's Falls, 69
St. Charles, MO, 94
St. Clair River, 55
St. Croix River, 69, 81, 111
St. Francis River, 83
St. Francis Xavier Cathedral (Vincennes, IN), 83
St. Francis Xavier Mission (MO), 86
St. Francois Mts., 85
St. Joseph, MI, 58
St. Joseph, MO, 87, 88, 89, 94
St. Joseph River, 28
St. Lawrence River, 69, 76
St. Lawrence Seaway, 20, 23, 65, 76, 104, 118
St. Louis, MO, 84*, 85, 86, 87, 88, 89, 91, 92, 93, 94
"St. Louis Blues" (song), 91
St. Louis Cardinals (baseball), 91, 93
St. Louis Center (MO), 93
St. Louis River, 69
St. Louis Symphony Orchestra, 89
St. Martin, Alexis, 63
St. Mary's River, 55, 66
St. Paul, MN, 73, 74, 79, 80
Stagecoaches, 93
Standard Oil Bldg. (Chicago, IL), 24

Standard Oil Co., 104
Starr, Belle, 89
Ste. Genevieve, MO, 86, 89, 93
Steam automobiles, 65
Steam shovels, 121
Steamboats and steamships, 8*, 17, 44, 52, 74, 93, 103, 117
Steel industry, 34, 37, 64
Steele, Franklin, 74
Steele, Theodore, 36
Stevens, Harry M., 105
Stevens, John, 119
Stevenson, Adlai E., 21
Storms, 46
Stowe, Harriet Beecher, 104
Straits of Mackinac, 58, 62
Strang, James Jesse, 60, 66
Strong, Phil, 49
Studebaker automobiles, 37
Sturgeon Bay, WI, 123
Suckow, Ruth, 49
Sugar Loaf Monolith (MN), 81
Summerfest, Milwaukee, 122
Sundew plant, 36
Superior Nat. Forest, 76
Superior-Duluth harbor, 111
Superior-Quetico primitive region, 81
Swan, Whistling, 1
Swedish settlements, 76
Swiss Settlements, 123
Sycamore trees, 36
Taconite, 76, 79
Taft, Robert, 106
Taft, William Howard, 48, 106
Taft Nat. Hist. Site, 108
Taliesin, 120, 123
Tama, IA, 43
Tama County, IA, 47, 48
Tank Cottage (Green Bay, WI), 123
Taopi (chief), 75
Tarkington, Booth, 35
Taylor, Zachary, 91
Tecumseh (chief), 31, 32, 35, 102
Telegraphy, 45
Telephones, 37
Television, 23
Tennessee River, 117
Tenskwatawa (The Prophet), 30*, 32, 35
Territory of Minnesota, 74
Thaquamenon Falls, 55*
That's Curious, 13, 15, 19, 23, 25, 28, 31, 32, 34, 36, 38, 41, 44, 46, 48, 49, 50, 53, 57, 58, 59, 60, 63, 67, 69, 74, 77, 79, 85, 86, 89, 90, 91, 92, 101, 102, 105, 106, 108, 109, 113, 115, 117, 120, 123
Thom, Robert, 91
Thompson, Virgil, 91
Tilden, Samuel J., 89, 105
Tippecanoe, IN, 35
Tippecanoe River, 32
Tires, 107
Tobacco, 67
Toledo, OH, 60, 97, 103, 108
Tornadoes, 46
Tractors, 51
Traer, IA, 49
Trans-World Airlines (TWA), 92
Transportation, 18, 23, 37, 38, 45, 46, 65, 66, 78, 91, 93, 97, 103, 105
Trappers and trapping, 58
Traverse City, MI, 66
Travois, 72
Treaties, 32, 74, 101, 102, 103
Treaty of Green Ville (Greenville), 102
Treaty of Paris, 74

Trees, 36, 41
Truman, Harry S., 49, 89, 90, 91, 94
Truman Library, 87*
Truman Sports Complex (Kansas City, MO), 94
Tulip poplar tree, 36
Twain, Mark (Samuel L. Clemens), 89, 91, 119
Twin Cities, MN, 79
Tying machine (grain), 119
Tyler, John, 33
Typewriters, 117, 119
U.S. Military Academy, 90
U.S. Steel Co. (USX), 37
"Uncle Tom's Cabin" (book), 104
Underground Railroad, 33
United Nations, 21, 63
University of Iowa, 45, 46, 49, 53
University of Michigan, 63, 67
University of Minnesota Mines Experiment station, 79
University of Notre Dame, 38*
University of Wisconsin, 118, 123
Urban Institute of Washington, DC, 79
Urban restoration, 93, 94
Valparaiso, IN, 37
Van Allen, James, 49
Van Allen belt, 49
Van Buren, MO, 83
Veblen, Thorstein, 78
Veiled Prophet Fair, 94
Verendrye, Sieur de La (Pierre Gaultier), 73
Vermillion River, 97
Veteran's Mem. Bldg. (Detroit, MI), 66
Victoria of England, 50
Vietnam War, 35
Viking explorations, 72
Villa Louis (Prairie du Chien, WI), 124
Vincennes, Francois de, 30, 38
Vincennes, IN, 16, 30, 31, 38
Virginia City, NV, 91
Vitamins, 119
Volcanoes, 71
Vollrath Co., 122
Vonnegut, Kurt, 49
Voyageurs, 30, 58, 73, 74, 77
W H A Radio (Madison, WI), 123
Wabash, IN, 33, 35
Wabash River, 13, 28, 30, 32
Wabash and Erie Canal, 32
"Walk-in-the-Water" (steamboat), 103
Wall Lake, 41
Wallace, "Uncle" Henry, 48, 49
Wallace, Ben, 39
Wallace, Henry A., 49
Wallace, Henry C., 49
Wallace, Lew, 35
"Wallace's Farmer" (magazine), 49
Walnut Hill, IA, 53
War of 1812, 16, 32, 44, 59, 74, 87, 102, 115
Ward, Aaron Montgomery, 21, 64
Warren, A. C., 59
Washington, D.C., 120
Washington, George, 31, 35, 46, 90, 101, 102
Washington, Harold, 21
Washington Island (WI), 111
Water Tower (Chicago), 11*
Water routes, 18, 23, 37, 39, 60, 73, 86, 93, 97, 103, 104, 113, 115
Water supply, 22, 55
Waterfalls, 55*, 69, 80, 124
Waterloo, IA, 51, 53
Watersheds, 28, 69, 83, 97, 104, 113

Watertown, WI, 116
Wausau, WI, 121
Wayne, (Mad) Anthony, 31, 59, 102
Wayne, John, 50
Wea Indians, 87
Weapons, prehistoric, 57
Weather service, U.S., 119
Weiser, Conrad, 100
Welsh settlements, 123
West Branch, IA, 47, 48, 52
West Point Academy, 90
"Western Engineer" (steamboat), 44
Western Reserve, 102
Westminster College, 94
Westport, MO, 88
Westward Expansion, Museum of, 93
Weyerhauser, Frederick, 77
Wheat, 79
White River, 83
Whiting, IN, 37
Wigwam (Chicago, IL), 18
Wigwams, 72
Wild West and Rough Riders Show, 50
Wild rice, 72*, 78, 114, 121
Wildlife, 22, 50, 64, 101, 120
Wildlife, prehistoric, 83, 85
William Rockhill Nelson Gallery of Art, 94
William Tell festival, 123
Williams, Andy, 50
Williams, Charles W., 46
Williams, Roger (entertainer), 50
Willkie, Wendell L., 35
Willow Run, MI, 62
Willson, Meredith, 49
Wilmette, IL, 24
Wilson, James (Tama Jim), 48, 49, 106
Wilson, Margaret, 49
Window in the stomach, 63
Winnebago Indians, 43, 114
Winona, MN, 6, 81
Winter Carnival (St. Paul, MN), 80
Wisconsin (main article), 111
Wisconsin Dells, 123
Wisconsin Hist. Soc., 123
Wisconsin Idea, 117
Wisconsin River, 43, 52, 73, 113, 115, 123
Wisconsin's Eagle Regiment, 117
Witness trees, 120
Wolverines, 64
Women's rights, 50
Wood, Grant, 49
Wood Lake, MN, 75
Woodland Indians, 43
Woodland Man, 85
World Series (baseball), 118
World War I, 20, 33, 39, 46, 47, 61, 63, 76, 89, 90, 104, 118
World War II, 20, 34, 47, 62, 76, 89, 90, 104, 118
World War Mem. Plaza (IN), 39
World's Columbian Exposition, 123
World's Fairs, 20, 89, 106, 119, 123
Wren, Christopher, 90
Wright, Frank Lloyd, 24, 119, 120, 123
Wright, Harold Bell, 49
Wright Brothers, 66, 104, 106
Wyandot Indians, 28, 100, 101
Yerkes Observatory (Lake Geneva, WI), 122
Zanesville, OH, 107, 109
Zebulon Pike Locks (IA), 52
Zinc, 92, 120, 121
Zoar, OH, 103
Zoos, 23, 67, 93, 109

ACKNOWLEDGMENTS

Maps, charts and graphs, EBE; Chicago Convention and Tourist Bureau, 3; Chicago Hist. Soc., 6, 7, 15, 30, 59, 72; Travelers Insurance Co., 8; Architect of the U.S. Capitol, 10, 11 (upper), 118; Allan Carpenter, 11 (lower), 66; Wisconsin Div. of Tourism, 12, 114, 122; USGS/NHAP/EROS, 14, 29, 42, 56, 70, 84, 98, 112; Stuart Collection, EBE;, 18, 19, 36; R. Laurent, 24; Illinois Dept. of Commerce, 55, 68; Michigan Bell Telephone Co., 61; Ford Motor Co., 63; Minnesota Dept. of Economic Development, 73; Minnesota Office of Tourism, 78, 80, 82; Missouri Div. of Tourism, 86, 87, 94, 95, 96; St. Joseph Museum, 88; Ohio Office of Travel and Tourism, 97, 110; University of Michigan Museum 100; Greater Cleveland Growth Assn., 109; U.S. Postal Service, 107; Wisconsin Dept. of Natural Resources, 111; Milwaukee Public Museum, 114

Ida Middle School
Ida, Michigan

Ida Middle School
Ida, Michigan